# Industry Regulation and the Performance of the American Economy

**Also by Paul MacAvoy**

*Explaining Metals Prices*

*Privatization and State-Owned Enterprises: Lessons from the United States, Great Britain, and Canada*

*Energy Policy: An Economic Analysis*

*Crude Oil Prices: As Determined by OPEC and Market Fundamentals*

# Industry Regulation and the Performance of the American Economy

Paul W. MacAvoy

**W. W. NORTON & COMPANY**
NEW YORK LONDON

The text of this book is composed in New Baskerville with the display set
in New Baskerville Bold
Manufacturing by Haddon Craftsmen
Book design by Suzanne Bennett

Library of Congress Cataloging-in-Publication Data

MacAvoy, Paul W.
    Industry regulation and the performance of the American economy /
by Paul W. MacAvoy.        p.      cm.
    Includes index.
    1. Industry and state—United States.   2. Trade regulation—United
States—Economic policy—1981–    I. Title.
HD3616.U47M275    1992
338.973—dc20                                                    91–31609

ISBN 0–393–96186–9

W. W. Norton & Company, Inc., 500 Fifth Avenue,
New York, N.Y. 10110
W. W. Norton & Company Ltd., 10 Coptic Street,
London WC1A 1PU

1  2  3  4  5  6  7  8  9  0

# Contents

# Preface

In its first one hundred years, regulation focused primarily on the communications, transportation, and energy industries. Starting with the Act to Regulate Commerce in 1887, regulation was looked on as the mechanism for solving public policy problems caused by arbitrary pricing and service practices of dominant companies in those industries. The companies used their market power to set prices in excess of costs and to discriminate against classes of consumers. Where two or three companies existed in the same market, rate wars sporadically broke out, so that prices varied over time from monopolistic to competitive levels. Given this state of affairs, regulatory commissions were set up to hold prices to cost levels and to end discrimination, as well as to stabilize prices.

Yet even as they were being put in place as the means to achieve "reasonable" prices, these agencies were given further, conflicting responsibilities, such as to extend service to favored groups of consumers and to protect the regulated companies themselves from the incursions of competition in some or all of their markets.

During the 1960s, regulation took on a comprehensive, new function. Agencies with sweeping regulatory authority were set up to increase the safety of both products and working conditions in manufacturing and to improve the quality of the environment throughout the country. By the 1970s, one or another agency had so much control over the prices, quantities, or methods of producing goods and services that the regulated industries provided more than one fifth of the gross national product. But in this same decade, both consumer groups and companies actively campaigned for the deregulation of many and various markets in transportation and energy where firms were still subject to price controls. With a century now of hindsight and a decade since the first wave of deregulation, a good question to ask is whether regulation can be made to operate more in consumers' interests.

The answer is developed at length in the five chapters of this book. In general, at its zenith the control system was not productive, tending to be restrictive in its effects on the growth of production and trade. The agencies in the transportation and energy industries held price increases below cost increases throughout the high-inflation business cycles of the 1960s and 1970s, preventing the regulated companies from earning sufficient returns to expand investment. The agencies overseeing the industries subject to health and safety regulation set standards that greatly increased production costs, and the higher costs were passed on in high rates of industry-specific price inflation. Holding prices to levels that were too low in the utility industries and compounding price increases in the new health- and safety-regulated industries reduced the growth of capacity and production throughout the economy in the 1970s and early 1980s.

This book sets out a fairly elaborate explanation for this pattern of regulatory and company behavior. One rationalization is that the results of the 1970s were the necessary product of a rigid regulatory system encountering extraordinary business cycle conditions or extraordinary policy demands for health and safety. An alternative argument is that the agencies themselves developed policies destined to generate such poor results in response to interest groups impinging on their activities. The descriptions of both process and policy in chapters three and four help to sort out the extent to which each explains agency failure.

Regulatory reform in the late 1970s brought an end to the adverse effects of price controls in transportation. The escalation of costs in the industries most subject to health and safety controls abated as well. But price controls in some of the energy industries and in communications continue in even more complex forms, with unknown effects, and new 1990 Clean Air Act regulations may impose even higher cost increases on manufacturing industries. It is important to determine whether such changes contribute to the economic slowdown created by regulation so that additional reform would be productive policy for this country. These are concerns in chapters three and four and come up as well in the general review of policy in chapter five.

The book is based in part on studies described in *The Regulated Industries and the Economy* published by W. W. Norton & Company in 1979. After proposing that I might want to update that work with a second edition, Drake McFeely of W. W. Norton went on to suggest that I consider anew both past and current effects of regulation on the economy. In response I began updating the earlier book, but my reading of the new results of regulation in the late 1970s and of deregulation in the 1980s expanded the book to such an extent that it has taken a new title and a life of its own.

Still, this study of regulation is not complete. There should be findings that explain the collapse of savings and loan banking in the late 1980s and commercial banking in the early 1990s, and that testify to the particularly adverse effects on bank performance of partial deregulation. Such research has not been reported on here. Similarly, other regulatory processes that are growing rapidly, such as those regarding medical services and employment conditions, will have to be analyzed and reviewed elsewhere to complete our knowledge of the interactions of industry regulation and the growth of the American economy. The excuse for not doing so here is that the results of price and safety regulations are now the most important even if they are not comprehensive.

My research and writing have been funded by grants from

the Sloan Foundation and the John M. Olin Foundation. In particular I want to acknowledge the support of Professor Albert Rees of Princeton University, who took a substantive interest in my proposal when he was president of the Sloan Foundation, and of Dr. James Piereson, executive secretary of the John M. Olin Foundation. I am grateful to Professor G. William Schwert of the University of Rochester for assistance in research design and to Professor Robert Pindyck of the Massachusetts Institute of Technology, as well as to Professor Merton Joseph Peck of Yale University, for providing many suggestions toward improving the manuscript. My gratitude to Teri Foley for numerous processings of the manuscript is unlimited. This book is dedicated to the John M. Olin fellows at Yale University and the University of Rochester with whom I have worked over the last two decades on studies of the effects of regulation. They include Mark Austin, Roger Bredder, Andrew Carron, Anders Eggen, Stephen Felgran, Patricia Gray, Lori Hatton, Eric Leavitt, Eric Mankin, Betsy Nichols, Lauren Rockwood, Laura Scher, Curtis Spraitzar, Kenneth Stanton, Craig Stewart, and Dean Weaver. Wherever they may be, as young executives, lawyers, and economists, I hope that they now look at regulation as a means of solving industry problems with an understanding of its limitations.

# Industry Regulation and the Performance of the American Economy

# 1
# Introduction

AFTER DECADES OF RELIANCE on regulation as the antidote to market imperfection, economists have come to question its effectiveness. Not only is there concern that regulation is failing in the goal of protecting certain groups of consumers, there is also an impression that it may be a leading cause of reduced economic growth rates. Reform is underway; the revitalization of investment in regulated, infrastructure industries is a leading theme of the movement to reduce controls imposed by commissions, boards, bureaus, and agencies of government.

Before embarking on this rendering of the regulatory experience, a few words on perspective are needed. To begin with, regulation has for the most part been founded on the best of intentions. To be sure, there have been cases in which companies have convinced governments to regulate them to prevent competition from breaking out in their markets or to protect themselves from having to meet more exacting safety standards on their own. But the general rationale for regulation has been that it provides protection for consumers or workers. The profit controls and price ceilings on electricity and telephone companies in the first quarter of this century were imposed to protect the consumer from the full exertion of monopoly power. General safety codes for the workplace and limits on smokestack emissions in factories promulgated in the 1970s were instituted for the protection of the health of workers and of the neighbors of these facilities. Even when special interests were supposed to be served by a new agency, such as the airlines by the new Civil Aeronautics Board of 1938, the general interest was not to be made worse off as much as it was to share in the regulations-augmented growth of that industry.

The policy problems to which regulation has been applied over the last one hundred years have been of some importance to the economy. Companies with market power raised prices in the energy, communications, and some transportation markets. And without policies to change strictly private incentives, firms may very well have discharged more pollutants into the environment than was socially desirable. Finally, plant safety was often impaired because workers and employers were ignorant of the hazardous conditions causing accident rates.

The question for any study of regulation, then, is not whether the problems are real, but whether regulation is the correct response. To a great extent, our reliance on regulation is a matter of history that can be traced back to the effort to curb market power. The traditional policy was to have a regulatory agency set price ceilings in line with the costs of production and distribution. Concern about the deterioration of the environment and about worker safety resulted in the application of regulation to these areas as well. The Environmental Protection Agency and the Occupational Safety and Health Administration have been established to set emission levels and equipment-safety standards, and to enforce them.

Regulation, however, is not the only way to deal with such market failures in a number of important cases. Indeed, policies to reduce barriers to entry, such as tariff reductions or antitrust actions, work better in dealing with monopolies in manufacturing and may work just as well as regulatory price controls in energy and transportation. The most recent direction of policy to protect the environment has been towards imposing taxes or fines on polluters, rather than towards expanding regulatory agencies' specifications for clean equipment. These are exceptions applied only to certain industries, however. Regulation has remained the standard way of dealing with the problems of imperfect competition and of adverse neighborhood effects from production.

Where regulation has run into trouble, one of two culprits has been often at hand. The first has been the practice of trying to please too many masters. In recent years, legislative directives have required more diverse and even inconsistent regulatory results in response to the demands of special interests.

From the beginning, of course, interest groups have been able to direct regulatory practices toward results for their benefit. While the Interstate Commerce Commission was set up in 1887 to "secure equality, so far as practicable, in the facilities for transport afforded and the rates charged by the instrumentalities of commerce," an important source of political support for equality was eastern farmers seeking higher rail rates for those farther west (see MacAvoy, 1965, pp. 110–11). Thus, it mattered less to an important political faction that rail rates were above costs, than that rates from Chicago were higher than those from Pittsburgh for commodities shipped to the East Coast. The resulting controls led to rates that varied more with the distance from the shipment's origin, but that were on average higher than before the advent of commission operations.

As the number of factions demanding services from the regulatory agencies has increased, the distortions produced by the regulatory process in both price levels and structure have become more pronounced. It was not the pure avarice of influential buyers that led to regulatory policies to maintain stable prices in utility and transportation markets during economy-wide high inflation. Nevertheless, both organized subgroups and those seeking to protect the general interest tried to maintain price stability in the economy by more severe use of price controls than justified by costs in the regulated industries.

The second culprit has been the limited level of managerial competence in the regulatory agencies. As the various agencies were established and their operating practices were refined, certain methods for regulating became widely accepted. These simple rules had characteristic results in keeping with the goals of regulation, but only under quite simple market conditions. Consider the use of ceilings on prices in line with previous period costs of service. They worked well when industry demands increased and costs decreased each year from larger scale. But when inflation was accompanied by recession, so that costs increased rapidly, this same method had quite the opposite effect. Prices lagged behind costs so long as costs increased continuously. The operating practices of the agencies by themselves generated adverse price and production behavior.

With intentions to serve the public interest modified (or distorted) by the demands of interest groups and by compromises to establish simple operating practices, what then has been the impact of regulation? The results to date are documented in chapters three and four. But without going into detail, these imperfect procedures have probably prevented regulation from working in the interests of consumers, by reducing production across the regulated industries and thereby reducing the rate of growth of the economy. Disappointment with these results between 1975 and 1985 spurred the movement for reform of regulation and, in the extreme, for deregulation.

There was more than just conservative political action motivating this movement. The Reagan administration carried on an effort that had been initiated as early as the Ford administration but that had reached its zenith with deregulation of airline, trucking, and railroad services in the Carter administration. Reform extended to court rejections of monopoly control of telephone services under agency regulation. Reform also has included policies to contain agency expansion by requiring that new regulations be cost-benefit justified in the federal budget process. Altogether, the reform movement was broadly based politically and covered many aspects of regulation, because it was a response to a general malfunction of the regulatory process.

At the same time that regulation has grown unattractive, there have been important improvements in other systems for public control of industry. Court procedures for assessing damages have developed to such an extent that companies that discriminate or impose environmental costs now have to anticipate adverse effects from the detection and exaction of penalties. While not perfect, the legal framework works so much better in the 1990s than when regulation was initiated in the 1890s or 1930s that it has become a much more attractive alternative to regulatory controls and practices.

The alternative of no policy at all has also become more attractive. The development of more efficient small-scale distribution networks and the vast expansion of the capacity of financial intermediaries have reduced barriers to entry into those industries where a few firms have traditionally been responsible for most of the final sales. Market power exercised by one or a few firms now would appear to be more effectively thwarted by new competitive entry than by regulatory limits on price levels. Similarly, private decisions to install new safety and pollution-control equipment work better if tax incentives are put in place.

The most immediate alternative is neither continuing with the current practices of the agencies nor starting on a campaign for widespread deregulation. Rather, it lies in decontrol of those markets now competitive or relatively free of neighborhood effects where significant reductions in agency controls would improve industry performance. Indeed, steps are being taken in electricity and gas distribution to eliminate the regulation of just those parts of production and transportation that would be competitive on their own. Measures are also being taken to reduce the extent and complexity of regulation for many producers by spinning off those operations subject to competition into separate, unregulated companies.

The remaining controls to which companies would be subject would be required to meet new standards for both sophistications and effectiveness. One such new method calls for price ceilings varying with general price inflation and with cost-reduction rates specific to the company. The limited scope of regulatory procedure would be accompanied by a new focus on sharing the benefits from cost reductions, with profits to producers and price reductions to consumers. Thus, reform would result in agency procedures setting the level of prices only where there is market power, such as in retail distribution of electricity, and when company cost reduction rates fall short of industry benchmark rates.

Revitalization could take other paths. Improving health and safety regulation requires that it be made effective in reducing various hazards. To do this would be to turn regulation away from writing and enforcing rules regarding what equipment can be used in controlling emissions and towards setting limits on the output of harmful substances. Basic regulatory structures in the 1990 Clean Air Act do take that step by specifying limits on sulfur emissions by each of the power plants in the eastern part of the country. More emphasis on plant emissions, rather than on the stack emission control device, would refocus attention onto the effectiveness of controls. To the extent that regulations specify performance levels, with regard to current technology and costs, the regulatory process would control benefits and come closer to realizing the intended results and to doing so within reasonable time periods.

There are other options, the most provocative being the abolition of all regulatory statutes, organizations, and interest groups. How far we should go towards abolishing the agencies depends on the extent of the harm they have done to the economy and the extent to which they can be improved. Have the agencies significantly reduced production? Have these results been so adverse to economic growth that corrections in the regulatory process would not be enough? These are the questions to be asked in the next three chapters. The answers indicate that trying to do too much, for too many groups, with cumbersome systems of public management have indeed led to substantial economy-wide losses. Whether this country should turn toward complete deregulation or even then only go part way is the subject of the last chapter.

# 2
# The Nature and Extent of Industry Regulation

ALTHOUGH GOVERNMENTAL CONTROL OF industry and trade dates from the state-mandated limits on road tolls and grain storage charges of colonial times, national regulation of specific industries began little more than one hundred years ago. The Act to Regulate Commerce (1887) marked this beginning, establishing the Interstate Commerce Commission to control railroad rates throughout the nation. State governments, following the lead of Wisconsin and New York, set up agencies before the turn of the century to control both transportation companies and utilities within their borders. After a surge of legislative activity in the economically disruptive 1930s, the federal and state regulatory agencies together controlled prices of energy (electric and gas), transportation (railroads, trucking, and airlines) and communications (telephone and telegraph) throughout the country. They also controlled entry and some aspects of pricing by financial institutions, and entry but not pricing in radio and television broadcasting. Only the legislative wave of deregulation experienced in the 1980s pushed back the extent of these controls, so that they now no longer encompass all of these industries at the federal level.

The agencies have had in common certain practices not identified with those in other governmental organizations. They have determined whether companies in these industries could legally provide service. Derivative from this granting of the franchise, they have invoked a case-by-case procedure of analyzing financial accounts to approve "just and reasonable" price schedules for individual companies. Although such setting of the tariff makes up the central core of regulation, other agency reviews of service quality have followed. Of course, there have been various adjustments to tailor regulation to specific industry conditions. The transportation, banking, and other agencies dealing with many firms in the same market have gone to capping prices at levels consistent with average operating costs across firms. In the 1960s and 1970s, this price cap system was extended first to natural-gas and then to crude-oil production, as Congress put in place regulations to limit price increases across all the companies responsible for production in designated fields. The price-ceiling process has been adapted further by new agencies setting limits on doctor's and hospital's fees reimbursed by health insurance.

The important new regulatory policy of the last two decades was the development of health, safety, and environmental regulation. The regulating authority for provision of service was extended to cover companies in manufacturing as well as utility industries. Rather than pricing requirements, the agencies designated the methods or the equipment to be used in production. Although it began in meat packing and pharmaceuticals in the first third of the century, this regulation was extended to durables, chemicals, petroleum, and other manufacturing industries in the late 1960s to meet environmental quality and workplace or product safety requirements.

But as health, safety, and environmental regulation expanded across the economy, price controls receded. Urged on by broadly based antagonism to energy shortages and declining service in transportation, as well as by the industries subject to price regulation in the 1970s, Congress and the courts reduced federal controls in energy and transportation.

The reductions went beyond making midcourse corrections to eliminating regulation entirely in some markets and curtailing it in others served by these industries.

The Ford administration in the mid-1970s went so far as to propose legislation to eliminate federal price-setting authority over airlines, trucking companies, natural-gas producers, and, spaced over five years, crude-oil producers. With one exception, that administration was not able to pass the necessary legislation. The Carter administration, at the end of the 1970s, successfully sponsored legislation to abolish federal price regulation of the airline industry and also to remove most of the price controls over interstate railroad and trucking services. In setting out its energy policy, the Carter administration passed legislation requiring the phasing out of price controls on natural gas at the wellhead by the mid-1980s.

The Reagan administration made further regulatory relief one of the four foundations of its new economic program for the first half of the 1980s. Price controls of oil products, still being phased out, were eliminated entirely by executive order early in that administration. More sweeping was the presidential order that required any agency promulgating a new regulation to bear the burden of proving that the regulation would improve the performance of the economy. Regulation in the old-line price-control agencies was further reduced, particularly in energy and transportation, by rule making in the agencies, in continuation of the policies of the previous two administrations.

Thus, the coverage of industry by regulation has both increased and decreased in recent decades. The patchwork of expanding and receding control systems was not national policy, but rather the result of numerous, separate actions by committees of the federal and state legislatures. This is not to say that we lack a substantial foundation for regulatory policy. The justification for price regulation of the utilities since the 1887 Act to Regulate Commerce has been to control prices of firms with monopoly power so as to increase the supply of goods and services throughout the economy. Particularly, regulation has focused on reducing prices in the infrastructure transport, communications, and energy industries to reduce downstream costs of manufacturing and trade throughout the economy. The transportation industries were also regulated specifically to reduce the discrimination practiced by imperfectly competitive companies against certain consumer groups, even if that regulation reduced competition. Regulation of health and safety was required to eliminate pollution and unsafe practices associated with "externalities," conditions in which firms used costly natural and human resources as if those resources were free to them and to the economy as a whole.

But even though regulation was justified in these normative terms, the actual control process has not worked to produce such widely corrective results. The costs in the last two decades from the regulatory process included more than those from dealing with a bureaucracy, extending to those associated with requiring that unremunerative service be provided to specific groups. Costs have greatly exceeded the economy-wide benefits from that process. President Ford in 1975 publicized that finding in his statement that regulation cost the economy more than $100 billion per year. Even though congressional reaction at that time was that "the estimate had substantial shortcomings,"[1] the thrust of regulation has indeed been to reduce the growth of the economy by that order of magnitude.

## Justifications for Regulation

The premise underlying long-established regulatory institutions was that they were to correct failures in market systems. That is, the commissions and agencies undertaking

[1]Staff paper (1975), pp. 58–140.

regulation were established to improve on the market system's ability to serve consumers' interests. What constituted failure was broadly defined by legislators and the press. In establishing regulatory controls over rate setting by the railroads, Congress responded to shippers' antagonism towards unstable and discriminatory cartel pricing, which had those shipping a longer distance paying a lower charge, paying summer rates that were half of winter rates, and enjoying actual charges discounted below official cartel rates. But the railroads stood to gain from controls, since long-distance rates would increase and competitors' discounts would become illegal.[2] Both trucking rates and airline fares were regulated because they were unstable, varying from monopolistic to competitive levels. In establishing regulation of the retail gas, electricity, and telephone companies, the state and federal legislatures held that local monopolies setting high and discriminatory prices were to be required to set cost-based prices. But all consumers should be able to obtain service as well. Prices to those consumers on the high-cost fringe of the market had to be set below direct costs to sustain the demand for such services. The commissions and agencies had then to protect the regulated companies from competitive entry that would erode the monopolistic prices that were charged to other consumers, so as to provide returns to cover this below-cost pricing to fringe consumers.

Regulation was supposed to have stabilizing effects. No matter the industry, regulation was established where it would prevent large increases in the prices of goods and services at any one time. The implication of stability was that companies licensed for service would offer prices that on average over a decade would be no more than sufficient to cover the average total (variable and capital) costs of service for all classes of consumers. With both averaging over time and over classes, regulation would then have one of two effects. It would either

[2]MacAvoy (1965).

reduce monopolistic prices or require that excess revenues from continued monopolistic prices to some consumers in some periods be used to subsidize services at prices below costs to other consumers at other periods.[3]

The most recent extension of regulation has been directed at industries in which health and safety conditions were thought to be below levels to maximize national product. The argument is that markets for clean air and safety are missing—there is not a price at which supply and demand for these services are equal. Important early initiatives of this kind were implemented by the Food and Drug Administration (1931) and the Federal Aviation Administration (1948). They served as examples for setting technical

---

[3]The company subject to regulation would be similar to that illustrated in Diagram one. With falling marginal costs (MC) and high fixed costs *(AC)* over the range of market demand *(DD)* so that no second firm could profitably enter, this company could set price. Its most profitable price is $p_0$ for sales $q_0$, and even though this combination results in excess of capital costs ($p_0 q_0 > AC \times q_0$), no second firm would enter the market since neither earns enough to cover *AC* at any output with only half the market demand. Regulation intended to use resources efficiently would set a price limit at $p_1$ for sales of $q_1$—where price equals marginal costs. But revenues $p_1 q_1$ are not sufficient to cover total costs (equal to the *AC* at $q$, multiplied by $q$, which is above $p_1 q_1$). A second charge has to be levied, such as a service charge mandated to obtain output, that compensates the firm for $(AC - p_1) q_1$. Alternatively, the single price has to be set between $p_0$ and $p_1$ to generate revenues to cover fixed costs. This brings the regulatory process into the pricing structure or else results in prices greater than the optimal $p_1$ level.

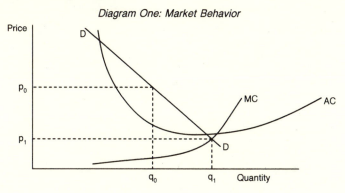

Diagram One: Market Behavior

operating standards or equipment requirements to improve the quality of service. Much more of this regulation was initiated in the 1970s, based on the argument that producers failed to take account in their costing and pricing of the environmental health and product-safety effects of their activities. The companies subject to such controls were expected to incur the costs of controls and were not to be compensated for these costs, even though from the perspective of the economy the quality of their goods and services was increased.[4]

But from the beginning the goals of regulation were not set out strictly as benefits for the consumer. The transportation companies, particularly the airline and trucking companies, were supposed to extend service by lowering charges below

[4]The basic policy goal is to close the gap in markets—to correct the failure—by acting as if common health and safety resources had been paid for by specific producers. In Diagram Two, the dotted supply curve $S_2$ is the horizontal sum of the marginal cost curves of all firms in the market after they have paid the common costs of natural and human resources they use in the production process. Rather than market price $p_1$ for output $q_1$, the regulator would impose costs or restrict output so that $p_2$ and $q_2$ result. Then prices are equal to full social marginal costs, and outputs (or GNP) are reduced to levels compatible with acceptable levels of the negative externalities. The benefits in higher quality goods are realized in the shift of demands to $D_2$ and in the final equilibrium at the same or higher output (shown here as $q_3$). But benefits would be realized as shown only if those buying these goods also realized greater environmental quality directly associated with that purchase.

*Diagram Two: Market and Regulatory Behavior*

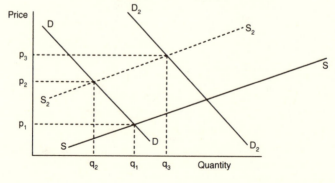

costs to some customers, so that they had to be assisted by the regulators in raising prices above costs to other customers. To maintain high price-cost margins on these other services required new entrants to be excluded from offering stand-alone service in just those markets, and this required further regulatory intervention.

Regulation was introduced into related industries to support service subsidies by regulated companies. Interstate Commerce Commission control of railroad rates had to be extended to cover the interstate trucking industry to prevent incursions from truckers into otherwise high margin rail freight markets for transporting mercantile goods. While the Motor Carrier Act of 1935 sought to "promote adequate, economical, and efficient service by motor carriers," it also set as a goal that regulation "develop and preserve a transportation system adapted to the needs of commerce," by controlling the split of freight tonnage between the rail and trucking modes.

Regulation was also supposed to prevent competition between regulated companies. The House report accompanying the Civil Aeronautics Act of 1938 set out that the purpose of regulation was to prevent high airline passenger fares but also to constrain "competing carriers from engaging in rate wars which would be disastrous to all concerned." Regulation was to bring an end to "this chaotic situation of the air carriers which has shaken the faith of the investing public in the financial stability and prevented the flow of funds into the industry." For the Communications Act of 1934 to be effective the regulation of the telephone industry by the Federal Communications Commission had to "make available so far as possible to all people of the United States a rapid, efficient, nationwide and worldwide wire and cable service with adequate facilities at reasonable charges." Making the system accessible to all users required that price-cost margins be low enough to bring in outlying consumers and yet high enough so that returns on existing

urban consumers were sufficient to cover system joint and
common costs. For this to be realized, there could not be
competing companies offering the same services to these
urban consumers at lower prices.[5]

In the extreme, the agency had to manage a complex
combination of competitive, collusive, stable, and nondis-
criminatory prices. To subsidize service in some markets, the
regulator had to restrict competing services in other markets, raising prices there towards monopolistic levels. Where
the industry was characterized by monopoly, this was to be
done by holding prices at monopolistic levels, using monopoly profits as the source of funds to subsidize below-cost
prices elsewhere. Where the industry was competitive, entry

[5]Thus, the documentation of the economic effects of regulation calls for examinations industry by industry of the regulatory tradeoff of consumer and company gains
from agency activities. These tradeoffs are addressed in Peltzman's theory of regulation, as in Diagram Three. Industry profits are maximized at $q_0$, the monopoly
output, and minimized at $q_1$, the competitive output. But the regulator trades off
more output for the consumer for more profit along political success frontiers $R_1$,
$R_2$, and $R_3$ to attain the highest frontier. This is achieved at $q_2$, the point on the
industry profit curve on the highest $R_2$, political success curve. If the industry before
regulation starts at $q_0$, then controls reduce profitability and should bring with them
company resistance. But if the industry was previously competitive and thus at $q_1$,
then regulation brings with it not only service obligations preventing the achieve-
ment of $q_0$ but also higher profitability. It would not be surprising in the latter case
to observe considerable willingness of companies to move forward into the regulatory sphere of influence. Cf. Peltzman (1976), pp. 211–240.

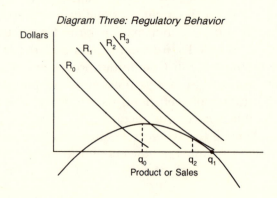

*Diagram Three: Regulatory Behavior*

and firm rivalry had to be constrained, so that some prices could be increased to generate the cash flow necessary to extend supply to fringe consumers, to have "available so far as possible to all people of the United States a rapid, efficient, nationwide service." Achieving that complex combination of prices that would satisfy all those consumers required systems beyond those developed in other parts of the government.

## The Extent of Regulation

What has been regulation's coverage of industry and trade in the economy? One measure of coverage is the amount spent by state and federal agencies charged with industry regulation. Their expenditures on personnel and operations to undertake case decisions and rule making, to conduct industry surveillance, and to carry out enforcement of decisions come to more than $10 billion per year.[6] But this amount is scarcely indicative of regulation's control of the economy. Indeed, the activity the regulators generate in the firms under their jurisdictions has involved more extensive outlays on personnel and operations than those in the agencies. More important, government expenditures on regulatory activity have initiated price and output responses over substantial parts of private-sector industry and trade, responses that have changed the annual rate of growth of national output in those sectors and for the economy as a whole.

The most important sectors subject to regulation are

[6]Total federal expenditures for social and economic regulatory agencies in 1988 was approximately $9.748 billion and in 1989, $10.146 billion (from *1989 Federal Regulatory Budgets and Staffing: Effects of the Reagan Presidency*, Center for the Study of American Business, 1988, Table A-1). To estimate state regulatory expenditures we sum state commissions' expenditures for those states that were available in the *1988 Annual Report on Utility and Carrier Regulation* (The National Association of Regulatory Utility Commissioners). Extrapolating from those states that provided data, the total state expenditures for regulatory agencies in 1988 was approximately $548 million.

shown in Table 2.1, with their shares of total gross national product (GNP). The retail sales of the telephone, electricity, and gas companies under the jurisdiction of price-regulating commissions have accounted for slightly more than 5 percent of total GNP throughout the last three decades. In the 1960s and 1970s the regulatory process also covered airlines and the interstate operations of railroads and trucking companies, and was extended to natural gas, crude oil, and petroleum products, so that another 6 percent of GNP was put under agency surveillance. The financial sector, accounting for approximately 3 percent of GNP, operated under controls on entry, service offerings, and interest rates at both the national and state levels. Counting both price- and entry-controlled industries, the share of GNP under regulation was as much as 15 percent in the 1970s.

**Table 2.1**

Percent of Gross National Product in the
Regulated Sector of the Economy[a]

| Category | 1965 | 1970 | 1980 | 1987** |
|---|---|---|---|---|
| Price regulation[b] | 6.6 | 12.1 | 11.6 | 5.3 |
| Financial markets regulation[c] | 3.2 | 3.5 | 3.4 | 3.4 |
| Health and safety regulation[d] | — | 14.5 | 12.0 | 10.9 |
| Total | 9.8 | 30.1 | 27.0 | 19.6 |

Source: National income and product accounts as updated by the Survey of Current Business (U.S. Department of Commerce).

[a]The calculations are industry-group gross product originating as a percentage of all-industry gross product originating. Industries are defined as including those companies or activities accounted for in the Department of Commerce's standard industrial classification.

[b]Includes railroads; trucking and warehousing; air transportation; telephone and telegraph; electric, gas, and sanitary services; and oil and gas extraction.   **Includes only telephone and telegraph; electric, gas, and sanitary services.

[c]Includes finance and insurance.

[d]Includes metal mining; coal mining; construction; paper and allied products; chemical and allied products; petroleum and related industries; stone, clay, and glass products; primary metal industries; and motor vehicles and equipment.

That these industries were the ones regulated raises questions about the simple monopoly rationale for policy. Regulation to correct market failures should be found where monopolistic practice otherwise would result in too little production and too high prices. Retail distribution of electricity and gas, and of residential or commercial telephone services, had for decades been provided by single companies in each community, so that a case could conceivably have been made for regulating prices in these industries. Even this limited case could not have been made for price controls in trucking or banking services. And from the beginning of controls, there were too many railroads or airlines between a city pair to produce monopolistic pricing, so the regulatory mechanism ostensibly was there to curtail competitive behavior. Oil and gas production was characterized by large numbers of suppliers in any field market so price regulation could only have been used to contain increases in competitive prices.

The reform of regulation during the Ford, Carter, and Reagan administrations stripped away substantial parts of the controls in these industries with less obvious rationale for regulation. The railroad, trucking, and airline passenger service industries were no longer subject to interstate price controls by the late 1980s. There still were entry and rate controls of intrastate trucking and limited controls over rail rates (on services where there was a single source of service for a large municipal or corporate customer), but as a first approximation these industries moved off the list of those generating GNP under regulatory regimes. Oil and gas extraction moved out of the regulated sector as well, as a consequence of "phased decontrol" in the late 1970s in legislation that eliminated price caps and allocations of supply to favored customer groups. Together, the reform initiatives reduced the regulated industry share by 6 percentage points, or to half of previous levels, of GNP.

The most significant advance of regulation, in terms of coverage of the economy, come about from the establishment of the agencies to increase workers' health or safety and to protect the environment. While such regulation covered virtually every industry, in practice, only some industries were required to adjust their pricing, production, and investment decisions significantly in order to comply with the regulatory process. Other industries were not as deeply affected, because their production processes were such either that virtually costless adaptation to the rules was possible or that costly standards did not apply. The mining, refining, and chemical industries were greatly affected by this type of regulation: substantial portions of their investment outlays in the 1970s and early 1980s were for equipment to meet regulatory requirements. The paper, primary metal, motor vehicle, and glass product industries were not required to make such extensive investments in plant and equipment, but they were as heavily regulated because controls on processes or products were important enough potentially to affect price and production levels. These industries together accounted for almost 12 percent of GNP.

Thus agency operations in pricing and in health and safety policy resulted in the regulated sector of the economy covering nearly 27 percent of GNP in 1980. This has been reduced to 20 percent, due to the elimination of important parts of price regulation and to the relative decline of GNP from the industries most subject to health and safety controls. But such a percentage is still large enough to raise questions about the way the economy has behaved because of the regulatory process.

To address these questions directly requires, first, a description of the methods used by the regulatory agencies to set prices and, in the case of health and safety regulation, to determine requisite methods of production and environmental quality. These methods have predictable results for industry price levels and production and ultimately for GNP.

## The Regulatory Process

How do the regulatory agencies actually control prices and production? The answer is of course both specific to the industry and at the same time generally the same across the controlled industries. Each agency, operating with a mandate appropriate for its industry, uses a generic process for determining whether the regulated company's prices are "just and reasonable" or whether that company's production takes place in ways that "protect the health of persons."

Price regulation begins with the agency's response to a company request for increases in its tariff schedule. Although the request generates divergent testimony and studies, in practice price-level increases have been based on recent period increases in operating and capital costs. In health and safety regulation, the request for a finding of in-compliance operation is granted if certain types of control equipment have been put in place. Thus, prices or production rights have been determined by agency findings on the characteristics of recent financial or plant operations.

There are two principal factors that make for uniformity of results across industries from this regulatory process. First, the various statutes establishing the many different agencies have been set out to achieve similar results. The goals in the Act to Regulate Commerce of 1887—stabilizing price levels and promoting uniformity in rail price structures—were repeated in later regulatory statutes calling for truck and airline regulation. The state and national statutes establishing agencies to control prices for electricity, gas, and telephone services all contain requirements for preventing high, unstable, and discriminatory prices as well. The new agencies controlling health, safety, and environmental conditions were called upon to solve different problems. But even there, similarity of statutory language calling for controls made them all require the use of equipment standards in regulated companies.

The second factor has been the Administrative Procedures

Act and its requirement that regulated companies have recourse to due process.[7] The procedures call for agency hearings in which presentation of evidence is subject to cross examination and in which findings on case decisions have to be justified by the evidence. By specifying that the courts determine whether the agencies have given due consideration to the evidence, this act has caused agencies to emphasize accounting data on past performance rather than judgmental or predictive assessments of what is reasonable. Thus, safety or pollution-control proceedings have focussed on recent plant production line results, taking little account of future costs or advances in technology. In addition, as the scope of judicial review has expanded over the last two decades, the issues on appeal have been extended to include whether, indeed, the decision of the agency itself was reasonable when measured against the goals of the statute.[8] To avoid unfavorable court reviews, then, the agencies have established procedures centering on facts and studies of past performance.

Thus price levels in public utility or transportation companies have been increased by the sum of changes in recent

[7] Cf. Administrative Procedures Act, 5 U.S. Code 551 et seq. and 701 et seq. (1976).

[8] As early as 1936, the Supreme Court (in *St. Joseph Stockyards Company v. United States*, 298 US 38 at 49–50 [1936]) said that "the Judicial inquiry into the facts goes no further than to ascertain whether there is evidence to support the findings, and the question of the weight of the evidence in determining issues of fact lies with the legislative agency acting within its statutory authority. But the Constitution fixes limits to the ratemaking power by prohibiting the deprivation of property without due process of law or the taking of private property for public use without just compensation." Thus the Court maintained the right to examine the weight of the evidence when allowed prices were alleged by the regulated company to be so low as to imply confiscation of its property. Present-day judicial practices have promoted to a much greater extent the Court's interpretation of the agency's legislative directives. This has narrowed and focused agency procedures, as indicated by Professor Stewart: "By undertaking a more searching scrutiny of the substantiality of the evidence supporting agency fact-finding and by insisting on a wide range of procedural safe-guards, the courts have required agencies to adhere more scrupulously to legislative Law" *Harvard Law Review* 88 (1975): 1,671, with reference to *Universal Camera Corporation v. NLRB*, 340 US 474 (1951) and *W. Y. Sung v. McGrath*, 339 US 33 (1950).

period (i) operating costs, (ii) depreciation, (iii) taxes, and (iv) reasonable profit. The first step has been to record "test period" operating costs and the second to determine from accounting records on relevant investments the capital base for depreciation and for taking the reasonable profit rate. The last step, finding the reasonable profit, has been arrived at by multiplying an agency-determined rate of return times this capital base. Judgmental elements have a role in agency determination of the allowed rate of return. But even there, the actual rates permitted by various agencies have been within a narrow range derived from a set procedure. The procedure relies on estimates of recent returns earned by investors in unregulated companies of comparable risk in the stock and bond markets or of current capitalization rates applied by investors to this company's earnings. On finding allowed rates of profit, then, historical data on recent actual rates have been the basis for decisions.

The agencies conducting health and safety regulation have developed an approval process that has a company in compliance when it has in place equipment meeting certain prior specifications. These pieces of equipment are expected to improve health conditions, operating safety, or environmental quality even though they are only one component in those aspects of firm performance. Indeed, in a number of instances, invoking standards has itself become the only goal of regulatory decision making. Even without that extreme, this regulation has achieved a degree of specificity in the physical conditions of production in manufacturing and mining.

## The Effects on the Economy

Over the last thirty years, between one-tenth to one-fifth of the economy has been subject to the regulatory process. The concern is with how this sector has fared. In general, the price-regulated industries have not performed as well, while the health- and safety-regulated industries have done even worse when compared to what could have been expected in the absence of controls.

There are numerous explanations. Extreme business cycle conditions in the 1970s and early 1980s disrupted operation of the simple systems used in carrying out price regulation. But at the same time, the regulators, when setting prices during these periods of simultaneous high inflation and recession, made decisions to keep price increases below the levels that in the course of earlier rate-making proceedings would have been found to be compensatory. In effect, agency-allowed price increases were smaller than those necessary to keep cash flow in line with increased operating and capital costs. With price increases less than those in other companies competing for the same resources, the regulated companies fell short of planned capacity expansion. At the same time, the resulting lower relative prices provided an incentive for more rapid growth in demands for regulated company service—demands that could be satisfied only so long as there was rapid expansion of capacity. By the end of the 1970s, the regulated industries, rather than leading in investment and production growth, lagged behind the rest of the economy.

At the same time, the industries most subject to health, safety, and environmental controls experienced larger price and smaller output increases, as if regulation had made production relatively more costly. Such a result may or may not have been adverse to the American economy; regulation was supposed to be beneficial as well as costly by reducing "bads" such as pollution and workplace accidents. But in general controls operated without significantly improving the quality of working conditions or of the environment. Given that the price increases in the most affected industries were quite large and that there were no general benefits, then this regulation had net adverse effects on the growth rate of the economy.

An examination of these effects of regulation in the last

thirty years is undertaken in the next two chapters. The results varied from industry to industry; some industries showed positive effects from price or environmental controls, but most suffered adverse effects throughout the 1970s. These adverse effects were reduced in the 1980s with lower inflation and less regulation. The prospects for improving further on the results of regulation are evaluated in the last chapter.

# 3
# Price Controls and Industry Performance

THE IMPACT OF REGULATION is largely determined by the way the agencies translate statutory goals into operating rules and case decisions applied to companies. Thousands of cases decided by each agency from the mid-1930s to the early 1960s established and more fully developed this process. As a result, the state and federal agencies controlling the energy, transportation, and communications industries had in place by the 1960s what were observably convergent procedures.

Under that regimen, the 1960s, with 2 to 3 percentage point price increases elsewhere in the economy, saw regulated prices remain almost constant. This was in keeping with the regulatory goal of price stability but at the same time kept profits on a par with returns in other industries. It was not repeated during the early 1970s. Significant increases in inflation in the rest of the economy made for differences in how the regulatory process affected prices of firms in regulated industries. That is, prices were kept substantially lower for regulated than for unregulated firms, causing reductions in relative cash flow with consequent long-run reductions in investment and output growth in the regulated industries.

The highly inflationary business cycle that characterized the middle and late 1970s exacerbated the effects from lag in price increases in the regulated industries. The concurrent high inflation and recession was not responded to in the regulatory process so that the regulated behind in acquiring the resources nece pansion and output growth. By the e higher rates of economy-wide inflation lated industries lagged far behind those in u. dustries or even those that could have been expected in u. industries if they were competitive. The pricing process did not adjust sufficiently to maintain industry growth in energy, in transportation, and, to a lesser extent, in communications. At least it is conceivable that other systems for controlling industry would have worked better—that is, would have made it possible for prices to have responded to demand and cost changes in these industries in the same way as elsewhere in the economy.

To develop these findings, we begin with a description of how price controls developed as a system. The common procedures used by the agencies are evaluated in terms of effects on prices in the low-inflation 1960s and then in the radically different high-inflation 1970s. Finally, the reduced regulation of the 1980s is appraised in terms of the growth performance of these industries.

## The Regulatory Process in Detail

Given the enabling acts of Congress and the state legislatures, the regulatory agencies have had and used the authority to determine all the important decisions of the companies under their jurisdiction. By rulings and by case opinions that further developed these rulings, they have specified whether companies could operate, what services they could offer, and the structure and level of prices they could charge. Some agencies have gone so far as to certify the kind of production equipment to be used, while others have decided whether consumer groups, or even individuals, had the right to demand service. A number of agencies have evaluated the oper-

ig performance of companies and the prudence of their
nvestment decisions. But these were exceptional. Most agencies have concentrated on determining "just and reasonable"
prices in the markets to be regulated.

They have conducted this key process in substantially the
same way. They have begun by requiring that the applicant
company be certified to provide service in a given area. For
the most part, certification prevented the development of
duplicate sources of supply in order to reduce the costs of
service, but it thereby also reduced competition. Usually this
process has stopped short of completely excluding substi-
tutes. For example, limits have been imposed that exclude a
second gas company from serving a metropolitan region, but
these limits have not totally prevented gas companies from
competing with fuel oil and even with regulated electric companies in the market for household heating. But certification
of entry into interstate trucking not only excluded many types
of competition among truckers, it also excluded competition
with the railroads in some types of bulk-commodity transportation (such as that from truck trailers on rail flatcars in the
1960s).

Certification involved more than just restrictions on the
number of suppliers. By acquiring rights to provide service
not granted to others, the regulated company gave up substantial discretion in its decisions as to whom to serve. Indeed,
the regulatory agencies in general have required regulated
companies to provide service they would not otherwise have
undertaken. For example, requirements to provide unprofit-
able rural services have been imposed on transportation, energy, and communications companies as part of the process
for obtaining approval of applications to serve more profitable urban markets.

After their certification process has established dimensions
of service, the regulatory agencies take the critical next step
of determining the level and structure of prices. This has been
done in response to company requests that the tariff be revised to allow certain proposed percentage price increases.

Requests have been granted, granted in modified form, or denied based on whether estimated revenues from the higher prices exceed recent increases in costs of service realized by that company.

Agency practice has been to make estimates according to the accounting equation in which recoverable costs $R = c + d + r \times B/(1 - t)$, where $c$ is total operating costs, $d$ is depreciation, and $r \times B/(1 - t)$ equals total allowed profit after taxes at the tax rate, $t$, and at the fair rate of return, $r$, on the net undepreciated capital investment base, $B$. The process of calculating $r$ and $B$ determines the results. Estimates of $c$ and $d$ have been developed from accounting data for recent test-period operations as a matter of course. But the determination of the rate of return, $r$, and the company's capital base, $B$, has involved lengthy adversarial proceedings in which agency officials choose among estimates by the company, the agency's staff, and consumer advocates. Small errors on the high side in estimating the rate of return can be compounded by multiplying by too large a rate base, resulting in a level of profits in the extreme equal to what would have been earned without regulation. But setting this rate below the company's current costs for capital in the equity and bond markets results in cash flow falling to levels that are insufficient to replace and expand investment necessary for maximum GNP growth. It is in determining $r$ and $B$ that the process succeeds, not only in regulating company pricing, but also in affecting the growth performance of the regulated sector of the economy.

The agencies have accepted estimates of the investment base as reasonable, in general, based on the original expenditures minus depreciation on plant and equipment specifically used in regulated operations. These estimates have been biased downwards when compared to replacement costs during periods of inflation, resulting in $B$ levels that were too low in the 1970s, for example.

There has been less uniformity in the process by which

agencies have arrived at allowed rates of return. They have acted on the premise that the companies should earn returns that made them able to compete in the capital markets for funds for the plant and equipment necessary for the growth of service projected to meet consumer demands.[9] Return rates have been set, based on the weighted average of the interest rates outstanding on the company's debt and an equity earnings rate equal to a multiple of the firm's common stock earnings/price ratio. The multiple of the earnings/price ratio that has been acceptable has varied from case to case and over time, not only because of changes in the condition of capital markets, but also as a result of pressure from intervenors in the rate proceeding for lower prices. The New York State regulatory experience provides an illustration. During the late 1960s and early 1970s, the regulated utilities in New York filed requests with the Public Service Commission for tariff increases based on the necessity for increases in their rates of return. The requested increases were larger the lower their common stock earnings per share and the lower their interest coverage ratios (income before taxes divided by total interest charges). Companies also requested increases at times when those allowed other firms under the Public Service Commission's jurisdiction were larger.[10] These factors turned out to be important in setting the allowed rates of returns, as was the size of the firm's request in total dollars of projected

[9]That is, an investor in stock of the regulated company always earns a rate of return equal to $(d + \Delta p/p + g)$, where $d$ is dividends as a percent of $p$, the stock price, $\Delta p$ is the change in stock price, and $g$ is the expected rate of growth of dividends. But the sum of these terms has to be at least equal to the same sum from investments of equal risk—the "cost of capital"—for investment in the regulated company to be forthcoming. The regulatory process can establish $d$ and promise $g$, but $\Delta p$ is not directly observable from earnings. Thus the commissions cannot depend on earnings data solely for estimates of costs of capital. See Myers (1972), pp. 58–97.

[10]Joskow (1972), pp. 118–40.

rate increase and the extent of objections from consumer groups.[11]

During the 1960s, the dollar amounts requested were small and objections by action groups were limited, so the allowed rates of return were close to those requested. When in the 1970s inflation across the economy brought with it requests for larger dollar increases, the profit rates allowed in New York increased, but were a smaller percentage of those requested. Most importantly, realized rates increased more slowly than did actual rates of return on investments elsewhere in the economy.

Although not all regulatory agencies used these factors in the same way, they achieved similar results on voluminous case loads in the middle to late 1970s and again in the early 1980s. The agencies maintained the allowed rates of return for three to five years at a time. When applications for tariff increases clustered together—as during the middle and late 1970s, periods of sustained economy-wide inflation—there was a tendency for allowances to stay fixed, only to break through to a higher level when the difference between existing and requested rates grew to 4 or 5 percentage points. This kept regulated prices relatively fixed with annual increases at levels below those in other industries.

## Price Regulation in the 1960s and Early 1970s

During the 1960s, price levels in the utility and transportation industries were scarcely changed by regulation. The detailed studies of each industry, and a comparative analysis of the GNP price and product accounts of the most regulated industries, indicate only limited effects from the regulatory process. In general, if there was an impact, it was to set

[11]Joskow (1972), pp. 632–44.

regulated price levels too low, but not so low as to reduce industry investment and production.

## Industries Studies

Moore found that the regulatory process had insubstantial effects on the measurable price performance of investor-owned electric utilities. The estimated unregulated price level ranged from 105.7 percent to 97.6 percent of the actual regulated price; that is, some power companies would have charged prices as much as 6 percent higher, while other companies would have charged prices 2 percent lower had they not been regulated.[12] In a second study of electricity in the 1960s, Jackson found that price controls had not been a significant factor in determining the level of residential rates.[13] Together with earlier research based both on case and

[12]Moore (1970), pp. 365–75. The purpose of this study was to measure the effectiveness of regulation in reducing prices to residential users of electricity. A weighted average marginal cost was computed for sixty-two private electric and seven municipal companies, based on the average cost of production of the marginal plant. By regression analysis, the demands at various prices were estimated for each firm and, from these demands and marginal costs, estimates were made of profit-maximizing unregulated prices. The author then compared these hypothetical "unregulated" prices with actual regulated prices to assess the effectiveness of regulation.

[13]Jackson (1969), pp. 372–76. Using multiple regression analysis, Jackson measured the effectiveness of state commissions in reducing the average price per KWH paid by residential and industrial users by comparing regulated and unregulated utilities that served cities of 50,000 for the years 1940, 1950, and 1960. His equation included five determinants of electric rates: $AR' = ao + a1P' + A2y' + A3F' + a4H' + a5R'$, where $AR'$ is average revenue per KWH, $P'$ is population in cities of 50,000 or over served by the utility, $Y'$ is income level of the population, $F'$ is fuel costs, $H'$ is proportion of electricity produced by hydroelectric power, $R'$ is the regulation variable set equal to one when the utility is regulated and zero when unregulated. The coefficients of the regulatory variable were negative in all three tests for equations with $AR'$ computed separately for total sales, residential sales, and commercial and industrial sales. However, a statistically significant regulation coefficient was observed for total sales only in 1950 and 1960. For residential sales, regulation had a marginally significant effect on rates in 1960, but not in either 1940 or 1950. Regulation did have a significant impact on commercial and industrial rates: "The

statistical analyses, these studies indicated that regulation was not effective in reducing rates.[14]

Telephone regulation, split between the control of state public utility agencies and the Federal Communications Commission (FCC), did bring about changes in the structure of price from one service category to another. The FCC applied "continuous surveillance" to the revenues from operations of the national telephone network owned by the American Telephone and Telegraph Company. Because a substantial part of costs were joint or common for all types of service, rates for specific services could not be based on direct costs for that service. A cost-allocation scheme was developed by the regulators to attribute joint costs to various local and long-distance services. Regulatory policy changes in this "separations" scheme assigned larger shares of joint costs to interstate long-distance services, thereby allowing the state regulators to hold down increases in local residential charges.[15] The residential rate levels in fact were kept below the direct costs of providing some services. An appraisal made of the Illinois Bell Company's rate structure in 1967 showed that direct costs were at least twice the rate level for local calls, but were only one-sixth of rate levels for long-distance calls. Overall, rates that year were below those that an unregulated monopoly

regulation coefficient is significant for commercial and industrial sales . . . [suggesting] that regulatory commissions succeeded in protecting the interests of the industrial and commercial users whose demand for electricity is more elastic than the residential consumer and are less in need of such protection" (p. 376).

[14]See Stigler and Friedland, (1962). See also Davidson (1955) and Twentieth-Century Fund, (1948). Earlier reviews of this research literature were provided in Caves (1964) and in Cramden (1964), pp. 182–91.

[15]See Federal Communications Commission Report, FCC Docket 20,003, p. 768, where it is stated that "the telephone industry contends that so-called 'specialized' services presently generate revenues substantially in excess of their direct costs, which help to defray overall system costs and thus to maintain low rates for basic telephone service."

company would have set, with the exception being the charges on interstate services.[16]

Natural-gas pipelines were also subject to split regulatory jurisdiction, since they offered both regulated service to gas retailers and unregulated service to industrial consumers. In the late 1950s and early 1960s, their regulated were not significantly lower than their unregulated prices, once account had been taken of costs and demand differences.[17] An important reason for this result was the system of rules utilized by the Federal Power Commission. Joint-cost allocation took place according to the so-called Atlantic Seaboard Formula, which allocated $50 + .5x$ percent of the pipelines' overhead costs to the regulated sector (where $x$ was the percentage of gas sold to retailers). Application of this formula resulted in a price structure that would have been quite profitable in the absence of regulation, because such large proportions of joint costs were shifted to regulated sales for rate-setting purposes that the companies could charge monopolistic (i.e., unregulated) prices on these regulated sales.[18] Wellisz found that the formula reproduced the unregulated price level, but within regulated service categories was biased against large-volume industrial consumers, raising rates to them and reducing rates to home-heating customers.[19]

In general, regulation in the 1960s did not significantly reduce the prices set by the natural-gas, electricity, and telephone companies. With respect to changes both in level and the structure of rates, as Jordan concluded, "If regulation has

---

[16]Littlechild and Rousseau (1975), pp. 35–36.

[17]MacAvoy and Noll (1973), pp. 212–34.

[18]Wellisz (1963), pp. 30–41. Also see Wellisz (1962), pp. 65–78 and 145–56.

[19]In applying the formula in individual rate requests, however, the FPC frequently had to tilt the structure to keep the industrial user on the system, thus preventing systematic cross-subsidization of home consumers. Cf. Aman and Howard (1977), pp. 1, 122.

had any effect it has been limited, [and] slow in developing."[20]

This state of affairs was compatible with the political process inherent in commission actions. Consumer representatives, in the legislature or elsewhere, had no procedural basis for demanding retail price decreases. The companies did not apply for price increases given that reported costs also did not warrant them by commission standards. Indeed, up to 1965, reported costs per unit of sales were generally declining, and it was only in the late 1960s that costs were increasing enough for particular types of services to justify applying for price increases. But then the agency's responses were limited. Industry studies indicate that rate regulation led in that period to a new price structure in electricity and gas pipeline services, as the agencies held prices to retail consumers down, while allowing increases in line with reported accounting cost increases to industrial consumers.

The effects of regulation on price levels in the transportation industries were not different in kind but were greater in extent than those in the utility industries. In markets where regulation prevented entry, the surface carriers and airlines were able to raise their fares above levels that would have prevailed under open entry. Fares and rates without regulation would have been "from 9 to 50 percent lower than they were with regulation, with many differences in the long run exceeding 30 percent."[21] Regulatory premiums, to the extent that they increased company revenues, were used to cross-subsidize service on low-density routes but not to increase producers' profits.[22] That is, "the evidence is quite inconclu-

---

[20]Jordan (1972), p. 163.

[21]Ibid., p. 167.

[22]No mention is made as to whether higher fares reduced total revenues where demand was elastic. This appears not to have been the case in these industries at that time, except perhaps for railroad transport.

sive regarding whether regulation has raised the rate of return for these industries. The railroads were probably helped initially, but regardless of regulation, disinvestment is now painfully taking place in that declining industry. At the same time, with or without regulation, capital is being attracted by the airlines and motor carriers sufficient for them to expand rapidly in response to increasing demands and advancing technology."[23] The higher fares and rates provided incentives for expanding services, particularly for airline passengers, so that regulation channeled competition into extensions of service on both low- and high-density routes. Because of this artificial service competition, the profits of regulated firms remained comparable to those in other industries.

The Civil Aeronautics Board regulated passenger fare levels on the basis of industry-wide costs per passenger mile, so that the average carrier was supposed to earn zero excess profits. The board also controlled the rate structure, with the intent that substantial profit margins would be realized on long-distance fares to be used to subsidize local service.[24] These policies were justified on promotional grounds with

[23]Jordan (1972), p. 172.

[24]Promotion of service was ostensibly a major objective of regulation of the domestic commercial airlines. The Federal Aviation Act of 1958 (49 USC Chapter 1302 or: Public Law 85-726, Title 1, S. 102. Aug. 23, 1958, 72 Stat. 740.) required that the CAB discharge its duties in a way that considered the public interest and "the public convenience and necessity" but required (a) "encouragement and development of an air-transportation system properly adapted to the present and future needs of the foreign and domestic commerce of the United States," of the Postal Service, and of the national defense at the same time that it should (b) "recognize and preserve the inherent advantages of, assure the highest degree of safety in, and foster sound economic conditions in, such transportation." There was in the next subsection a requirement for the (c) "promotion of adequate, economical, and efficient service by air carriers at reasonable charges, without unjust discriminations, undue preference or advantages, or unfair or destructive competitive prices." The potential conflict was with the "development of an air-transportation system" that was larger than possible at "reasonable charges" and therefore required higher fares than those found in competitive markets or even under conditions of rate-base rate-of-return regulation in the public utility industries.

the board recognizing that "short-haul markets (were) alleged to be very price elastic because of competition from other modes, and thus the price must be depressed below average cost in order to expand markets. On the other hand, long-haul markets were allegedly less price elastic, making it possible to maintain fares above average costs without losing substantial traffic."[25] Use of the fare schedule as the means by which to expand service to small communities came at a time when federal expenditures to provide service to these communities were scaled down and finally eliminated.[26]

The case decisions of the Interstate Commerce Commission (ICC) moved towards realizing a rate structure in which operating profit margins were positive on high-density lines but negative on light-density or feeder-line service to small communities. This was forestalled by a "shift of [the] cost burden to [large volume] shippers by increasing carload freight rates,"[27] causing reduced rail tonnage shares on the high-density routes.

ICC regulation of interstate truckers set limits on trucking companies' profits as a percentage of sales, rather than as returns on a capital base. The commission controlled the truck rate structure to achieve some limited subsidization of smaller shippers. Working through company rate bureaus that forged collective agreements, the commission allowed the highest operating profit margins for shipments of goods on which there was little competition. In turn, margins were supposed to have been held down on service to smaller and more isolated shippers, but this was more in form since the commission did not strictly enforce the requirement to serve these shippers.[28]

[25]Douglas and Miller (1974).

[26]Caves (1962).

[27]Conant (1965), p. 132.

[28]Nelson (1965), p. 415–16, noted that "supporters of current regulation . . . strongly claim that it results in improved service, greater financial responsibility to

Was there then a systematic pattern of results from utility and transportation regulation? If there was it had to be separated from the effects of other factors working on industry pricing. Substantial changes took place in demand and costs across these industries in this period. But, after accounting for such conditions, the result from regulation across these industries was similar. Prices were not substantially reduced.

This could be explained as the product of the administrative process in working with poor accounting data while still attempting to set effective limits on prices. But Jordan argued that the result was consistent with regulatory policy designed to protect producers from the incursions of competition.[29] Even so, more than producers gained from regulation: Regulatory policies kept telephone services to home users at relatively low prices and feeder-line transportation rates low relative to other prices. Because of selective rate reductions, the regulatory process was given credit for having expanded service to some small communities. While regulation tipped the balance towards high price levels, it also provided lower prices for certain classes of final consumers.

### Regulated Industry Prices and GNP Growth in the 1960s

The economy of the 1960s, with inflation rates of only 2.3 percent and GNP growth rates of 4.1 percent per annum from 1960 to 1969, was especially conducive to price stability in the regulated industries. Prices in energy, transportation, and communications increased slowly during the early part of the decade, at annual rates less than those in the unregulated industries. The regulated companies took proposals for in-

shippers, and greater public safety on the highways. . . . Acknowledging that even regulated carriers prefer to serve points generating substantial traffic, the commission indicated that 'in some instances' it had imposed a duty of serving small intermediate points by including them in a carrier's certificate even though an authorization was not sought."

[29]Jordan (1972).

creases to the agencies infrequently during this period, preferring instead to maintain prevailing levels. During the last half of the decade, the results were even better, with prices not increasing at all under controls. Table 3.1 indicates that over the 1960–1969 cycle prices increased on average by no more than 0.1 percent per annum in the seven regulated industries, and in only one industry—the airlines—was there an increase greater than a percentage point per year.

## Table 3.1
### Price-Regulated Industries: Average Annual Percentage Change of Implicit Price Deflators

| Industry | 1960–1969 | 1969–1973 |
|---|---|---|
| Rail transportation | − 1.0 | 7.0 |
| *Cost index* | *3.0* | *11.5* |
| Airline passenger service | 1.3 | 6.7 |
| *Cost index* | *− 1.1* | *6.6* |
| Electric, gas, and sanitary services | 0.2 | 2.4 |
| *Cost index* | *0.4* | *4.0* |
| Telephone and telegraph | 0.1 | 2.5 |
| *Cost index* | *− 1.4* | *2.2* |

Source: National income and product accounts as updated by the Survey of Current Business (U.S. Department of Commerce) and gross product originating components and net capital stock from Bureau of Economic Analysis (U.S. Department of Commerce).

Computation: The cost index is equal to:

$$[(\Delta IPD_{ci}/IPD_{ci}) \times (TR_{ci}/TR_{ri}) \times (I_{ri}/I_{ci}) +$$
$$\{[(\Delta W/K_{ri}I_{ri}) - (\Delta W/K_{ci}I_{ci})] \times (I_{ri}/TR_{ri}) +$$
$$[(\Delta Q_{ci}/Q_{ci})(TR_{ci}/TR_{ri})(I_{ri}/I_{ci}) - (\Delta Q_{ri}/Q_{ri})] +$$
$$[(\Delta T_{ri}/K_{ri}I_{ri} - \Delta T_{ci}/(K_{ci}I_{ci})) \times (I_{ri}/TR_{ri})],$$

where *IPD* is the implicit price deflator; *TR* is the turnover ratio (the current income/net capital stock); *WK* is the wages to capital ratio (the current wage payments/net capital stock); I (the expected return on investment by industry) is the riskfree interest rate + Beta (marketwide return − riskfree rate) and the asset Beta in the covariance of the industry return with the total financial market return divided by the variance of the market return, adjusted for financial leverage; *T* is taxes; *ci* equals the comparative industry and *ri* equals regulated industry designation for firm or company *i*, and the comparative industry is all industries contributing to gross domestic product less the regulated industries.

Appearances might then suggest that regulation had been effective in containing price levels. But even though these industries did forgo price increases, this need not have been the result of regulation. If their costs were not increasing, then, even without regulation, prices would not necessarily have increased. Similarly, if their productivity of labor or capital increased at a greater rate than elsewhere, then their unregulated prices should have been reduced by more than prices elsewhere in the economy. In order to determine whether there was a regulatory effect, we must compare actual price changes with cost index changes. The standard implied by the comparison is that cash flow per dollar of investment should be maintained at the same level relative to other industries.

The index of cost change justifying a price change for any regulated industry is equal to unregulated industry cash flow per dollar of capital stock adjusted for relative changes in output, operating expense, and taxes. The index increases when prices elsewhere increase, but decreases if output elsewhere increases at a slower rate or if operating expenses increase at a slower rate than experienced in the regulated industry. This cost index of the regulated differential is adjusted for the relative risk of investment in the regulated versus the other industries.

Regulation should keep the net cash flow per dollar of capital of regulated companies stable relative to that of unregulated companies. Then this index can be used to measure excessive or deficient price levels. Solving for changes in the index for the regulated industry in terms of relative inflation, output, and operating expense changes by industry and year, the excesses of regulated price are as shown in Table 3.1.[30]

The table begins with two business cycles during the 1960s. In the first, operating costs in these regulated industries fell and output increased relative to industries elsewhere, so that prices whether or not regulated should have increased less

[30]The equation for calculation of the index is shown in Table 3.1.

than in the rest of the economy. Indeed, substantial relative growth in airline and telephone services resulted in negative index cost growth; in electric and gas there was no index cost growth. Only in rail freight, with no production increase, did the index grow at 3 percent per annum.

The cost indices imply three types of regulatory effects. Actual annual price changes for airline and telephone services exceeded the index changes, so regulation allowed excessive relative price increases of from 1.7 to 2.3 percentage points per annum. Annual price changes in the energy industries fell short of index increases, but by only .2 percent per annum. This difference is so small that the conclusion has to be that regulation had no effect in the energy industries. But prices fell 4 percentage points below cost increases each year in rail transport, so regulation seems to have kept prices down in rail transport. (Yet there is an explanation for the limited price increases in rail transportation other than regulatory constraint—cash flow was reduced because of declining demand for rail services, so index increases would not have been achieved even if there had been no regulation).

The pattern of price behavior changed in the regulated industries through the second of these two business cycles. During the 1969–73 period, when economy-wide inflation increased to 5 percent per annum, the regulated industries increased their rates or fares between 2.5 and 7.3 percent per year. But most if not all of the regulated prices increased less than they should have for cash flow parity with other industries. Actual prices, to keep up with the cost index changes, should have increased by 1.8 percent more in the energy industries and 5.5 percent more in rail transport each year than they did. Only airline passenger fares and telephone and telegraph service charges continued to increase in line with the cost index increases (and thus with cash flow parity to other industries). The conclusion is that for four of these seven industries in the late 1960s regulated prices were inflexible against economy-wide inflation.

Thus, findings on industry-wide price changes in the mid-

1960s support the results of the industry studies on the effects of regulation. Changes in the GNP accounts show that price increases in the 1960–69 cycle were at levels expected from parity with industry-specific cost increases and with general inflation, and the industry studies found that regulation had not reduced price levels in that period. While these findings look similar, they are not exactly the same—industry studies had prices at monopolistic levels, while GNP-related indices showed prices increasing at the same rates as elsewhere.

But prices in electric, gas, and rail transport were kept below levels compensating for cost inflation in the 1969–73 business cycle. At the end of that cycle, then, prices might not have been at levels equivalent to what would have been realized without regulation.

The question is whether cash flow per dollar of net capital stock was significantly reduced by regulatory pricing in these industries by the end of the decade. As indicated in Table 3.2, cash realized annually per dollar of invested capital in unregulated industries was roughly equal to that for other energy and telephone industries, but was more than that in the transportation industries over the 1960–69 cycle. Cash flow in the energy companies did fall behind, but by only 2 cents per dollar of net capital. The rail freight companies experienced substantial cash flow losses relative to the index level of 17 cents per dollar of net capital in other industries. During the high inflation years of the 1969–73 cycle, however, all the regulated industries except telephone and telegraph fell 3 to 10 cents behind in cash flow per dollar of capital relative to that in unregulated companies in other industries. By the early 1970s, investment cash flow in the regulated industries was below that earned elsewhere.

This should have led to reductions in the profit rate on equities held by shareholders in companies in the regulated industries. There are indications of some reductions, but again mostly at the end of the decade. The regulated companies' returns to stockholders, as shown in Table 3.3, indicate

## Table 3.2
### Price-Regulated Industries: Cash Flow per Dollar of Net Capital

| Industry | 1960–1969 | 1969–1973 |
|---|---|---|
| | (annual average, cents per dollar of net capital) | |
| Rail transportation | 5.4 | 5.5 |
| *Comparative index* | *17.2* | *16.0* |
| Airline passenger service | 18.8 | 12.8 |
| *Comparative index* | *19.3* | *17.6* |
| Electric, gas, and sanitary services | 13.1 | 11.6 |
| *Comparative index* | *15.1* | *14.4* |
| Telephone and telegraph | 17.3 | 14.5 |
| *Comparative index* | *15.5* | *14.7* |

Source: National income and product accounts as updated by the Survey of Current Business (U.S. Department of Commerce) and fixed reproducible wealth table for nonresidential private capital by industry, current-cost valuation (U.S. Department of Commerce/BEA); market returns calculated from CRSP database.

Computation:

Cash flow per dollar of net capital = turnover ratio × gross margin;
(gnp/average net capital) × (gnp − wages and supplies − taxes)/gnp) =
[(gnp − wages and supplies)/average net capital].

Comparative index for the nonregulated sector of the economy =
[(GNP$_c$ − wages$_c$ and supplies)/average net capital]
× (I$_{ri}$I$_{ci}$) as defined in Table 3.1.

that company profits from current and expected operations as capitalized by stockholders in stock price appreciation in the early 1960s were approximately equal to those in unregulated companies. Six of the seven regulated industries had returns only one or two percentage points less than would have been earned by an investor buying the market as a whole and adjusting that portfolio for relatively more or less risk than in the regulated industries (while the airlines, with greater price increases, but comparable cash flow and promising new jet engine technology, experienced stock-price increases four percentage points more than the market). All

## Table 3.3
### Price-Regulated Industries: Stock Market Returns to Shareholders of Companies in These Industries

| Industry | 1960–1969 | 1969–1973 |
|---|---|---|
| | (average annual percentage return) | |
| Railroad transportation | 5.3 | na[a] |
| *Comparable market return* | *8.0* | *na[a]* |
| Airline passenger service | 14.8 | −7.9 |
| *Comparable market return* | *10.8* | *0.9* |
| Electric, gas, and sanitary services | 6.4 | 0.3 |
| *Comparable market return* | *7.2* | *3.4* |
| Telephone and telegraph | 5.3 | 4.3 |
| *Comparable market return* | *6.9* | *3.6* |
| *Value-weighted market-wide return* | 8.2 | 2.7 |

Source: Center for Research in Security Prices (University of Chicago).

Computation: Annual compounding formula:

$$\{(1+R_{f1})(1+R_{f2}) \ldots (1+R_{fm})\} \times [12/n)]$$

where $R_t$ is the monthly value-weighted market return of a portfolio including price change and dividends and $n$ is the number of months.

Comparable market return for industry $j$ = riskfree rate + Beta (market return − riskfree rate). The equity beta is the covariance of the industry return with the market return divided by the variance of the market return.

[a]Na = not available; we were unable to construct a consistent series of rail company stock prices for more than six companies.

seven regulated industries had returns each year in the 5 to 6 percent range, except for the airlines, which had returns of 15 percent. But in the 1969–73 business cycle, four of the industries had negative or zero stock market returns, substantially below comparable (risk adjusted) market-wide rates of return. On the whole, in this second cycle, investors realized lower rates of return on the shares of regulated companies than on those of comparable unregulated companies elsewhere in the economy. In some cases, changes that occurred in regulation itself affected the investor's outlook. Prospects for returns on telephone company stock were adversely affected by a 1965 Federal Communications Commission investigation of AT&T's rate of return on long-distance telephone service. Generally, however, it was the reluctance of agencies and commissions to allow the price increases proposed by the companies that reduced cash flow and ultimately reduced the stock prices of the companies in these industries.

These lower returns had to affect investment, if not necessarily all at once. Regulation could have had the effect initially of bringing profits into line with capital costs by lowering prices from monopolistic to cost-of-service levels, causing investment and production to expand to meet the increased demand attendant upon the relatively lower price levels. But to the extent that regulation-reduced profits fell below capital costs, investment would have to fall while demands for output increased. In fact, regulation probably did cause investment in capital equipment to increase in the energy industries in the late 1960s, but it probably caused investment to decrease in the transportation industries. As shown in Table 3.4, investment growth rates increased from 3.5 to 5.0 percent per annum even in the face of low stockholders' returns during the second business cycle in the decade. With strong growth

### Table 3.4
Price Regulated Industries: Additions to Net Capital Stock

| Industry | 1960–1969 | 1969–1973 |
|----------|-----------|-----------|
| | (percentage annual rate in constant 1982 dollars) | |
| Rail transportation | −2.2 | −1.8 |
| Airline passenger service | 12.5 | 4.7 |
| Electric, gas, and sanitary services | 3.5 | 5.0 |
| Telephone and telegraph | 6.6 | 6.6 |
| All other industry | 4.0 | 3.9 |

Source: Net capital stock nonresidential, current cost by industry, from statistics on fixed reproducible tangible wealth (U.S. Department of Commerce/BEA).

in demands for electricity and gas service, these industries kept expanding. At the same time, investment rates in rail transport were negative at $-1.8$ percent per annum and in airlines were reduced from 12.5 to 4.7 percent. Investment rates of the telephone service companies remained constant at 6.6 percent per year over the two business cycles. This pattern suggests that regulation had only begun to reduce investment across the seven industries during the late 1960s by holding back on price increases that were necessary for compensatory profits.

Real GNP growth rates in these industries were consistently high. As shown in Table 3.5, production growth in the 1960–69 cycle in the regulated industries exceeded that in other industries, except in railroad transportation. Airline service grew at more than twice the economy-wide rate in the process of introducing jet airframe technology. Telephone service maintained its pattern of growing 5 percentage points more than economy-wide GNP. In the second cycle, from 1969 to 1972, the rates of growth for the transportation industries fell, with rail-transport growth becoming negative

**Table 3.5**
Price Regulated Industries: Real GNP Growth Rate

| Industry | 1960–1969 | 1969–1973 |
|---|---|---|
| | (annual percentage rate) | |
| Rail transportation | 2.2 | $-1.4$ |
| Airline passenger service | 11.1 | 4.6 |
| Electric, gas, and sanitary services | 6.1 | 6.3 |
| Telephone and telegraph | 8.1 | 8.6 |
| Gross domestic product less economic regulated industries | 3.9 | 2.7 |

Source: National income and product Accounts as updated by the Survey of Current Business (U.S. Department of Commerce)

Computation:

$$\text{Growth rate} = \{(\text{GNP}[\text{year}_{in}]/\text{GNP}[\text{year}_{i-1}])^{1/n}\} - 1;$$

where $n$ = number of years and $i$ = beginning year, in 1982 dollars.

and airline growth falling from 11 to 5 percent (a level still higher than that for economy-wide GNP). The energy and telephone utilities expanded production at earlier annual rates, even though economy-wide GNP growth was lower. Regulation operated to require companies to meet relatively large increases in demand, even when this demand was being stimulated in the late 1960s by annual regulated price compression.

## The Exceptional Case of Regulation of Natural-Gas Wellhead Prices

During the 1960s the Federal Power Commission (FPC) made an extensive effort to control the prices at which producers sold natural gas to the interstate pipelines for retail distribution. Given that most deliveries had to go to these pipelines, this regulation was effective in holding field prices on both local and interstate sales. The low prices led to increases in demands and also to decreases in supplies going into the pipelines. Inevitably, there developed a substantial shortage of natural gas.

The result was inevitable given the methods used by the commission. Wellhead regulation was initiated by the FPC after the Supreme Court held in 1954 that the commission had the responsibility to control prices on sales by gas-field producers to the interstate pipelines.[31] Prior to this, while there had been considerable controversy about whether regulation extended to field pricing, the FPC had not set limits on producers' prices. But with Congress unable to provide a bill granting a clear producer exemption, given the 1954 court decision, the commission established control of new contract prices.

Its first approach was to treat each producer as a public

---

[31] *Phillips Petroleum Company v. Wisconsin,* 225 US 625 (1954).

utility and to set prices on the basis of individual company costs of service, including operating costs, depreciation, and fair return. After some years of trying, it became apparent that the sheer volume of cases, involving thousands of contracts, made such an orthodox process impossible. The second approach was to set regional price ceilings. To accomplish this, the FPC in 1960 divided the Southwest into five geographical areas, set interim ceiling prices at the extant 1960 levels for new contracts, and initiated hearings to determine the final ceiling prices for each area. But through the 1960s, agency and court reviews resulted in permanent ceilings only for the Permian Basin of west Texas and for southern Louisiana. The first set of prices was slightly higher than the interim 1960 prices, and the second set for southern Louisiana was at the interim 1960 level.[32] Thus interim ceilings became the final prices for the full decade.

That the commission intended to do more than hold that price level was evident from the way in which price structures were specified in the decisions. It set two price levels in the rate proceedings, with higher prices on new gas (recently discovered and developed, but not yet committed to a specific buyer) and lower prices on old gas (already committed to a buyer). The higher prices on new gas were based on higher costs for finding and developing additional supplies. The lower prices on older supplies were justified to provide returns on average historical costs of developing reserves at an earlier time when such costs were lower. Thus, in the Permian Basin area rate case, the commission's staff surveyed the operating gas producers in order to find their costs of production for the base year 1960. Experts employed by the producers and the retail distributors made separate surveys, and provided a range of estimates of historical exploration and development costs per unit of new and old gas delivered into a pipeline. After considerable review of these estimates, the

[32]The reopening of the case late in the decade, however, raised the ceiling by 25 percent.

FPC set two price ceilings at the lower end of historical average costs for either old or new supplies.

What this process did was to invoke ceilings without a foundation. The provisional ceilings determined the development activity that produced the historical costs later that decade, and these historical costs, in turn, determined the permanent ceilings. If producers in the early 1960s surmised that they were unlikely to be able to sell gas at more than the interim prices, then they would develop only those reserves that had costs lower than these interim prices. This resulted in the average cost of new reserves being roughly equal to the interim ceilings (given no significantly good or ill fortune in development). Thus using these recent historical average costs to set future costs in effect amounted to using historical prices to set future prices.[33]

Fixing prices at 1960 levels resulted in gas below oil and coal price levels at most major consuming points.[34] This had the effect of increasing gas demand compared to other fuels, as did new environmental standards. As customers switched to gas and obtained connections to pipelines or retailers, the pipelines sought to contract for more supplies to meet the higher expected consumption draughts on their systems in the future. Although the pipelines sought the customary fifteen-year reserve backing for each annual increment of committed delivery, they failed to obtain these requisite commitments. In fact, had they gotten fifteen-year backing, the total

[33]The commission further distorted the price by using average rather than marginal costs. Natural gas produced from a limited inventory has always been increasingly more costly to obtain as reserves have been depleted, so marginal costs have to be greater than the average costs of finding and developing market supplies. Prices set equal to average costs fail to compensate for additional supplies, so exploration and development is cut back. The commission tried to prevent this and thus to take account of higher costs at the margin by adding onto the average historical costs of finding gas another premium for new discoveries. In the Permian Basin proceedings, this premium was approximately 1 percent per MCF in the ceiling price. This difference, while important in principle, was insubstantial in practice.

[34]This is after adjusting for oil and coal transportation costs, inventory costs, and thermal efficiency differences.

new contracts of producers to the interstate pipelines each year would have to have been for 21 to 24 trillion cubic feet. However, commitments were in fact in the range of 9 to 16 trillion cubic feet in the late 1960s. Thus demand was increasing at such a rate as to create reserve-backing shortages.

Producers had to provide gas for added consumption from existing committed reserves. This could continue for only a few years, and by 1972 there were not sufficient committed reserves to meet demands so that operating shortages began to occur. They brought about significant change in the regulatory process. In order to prevent disruptions from interrupted service, the FPC created priority rankings for customers that limited access to gas and required use of other fuels during certain periods. Thus the result of price controls in the 1960s was rationing in the 1970s.

The results could not have been avoided so long as the commission was operating with a goal of setting prices based on average historical costs. The sequence of reserve depletion, production shortage, and rationing had to follow from the commission's control practices. Prices based on average costs, rather than on the higher marginal costs of supplies expanding to match demands, had to cause supplies to fall short of demands. That effect was masked in the short run by increased production out of already committed reserves. Only when such inventory became one third depleted did shortages of production begin, and by the time these shortages arrived, it was too late to use market processes to adjust supply so that more regulation was necessary to allocate the deficient supply among excess consumers.

### Price Regulation during the 1970s

The regulatory problems in the natural-gas industry spread to the other price-controlled industries in the 1970s. To be sure, the increases experienced in costs against fixed prices were inherent in an industry in which lowest-cost inventories were used up first. Exploration resulting in reduced gas reserve discoveries each year made the costs of additional production always greater than the historical costs that set prices for this product. The utility and transportation industries also had begun to experience greater cost increases than price increases—not because of conditions inherent in the production process, but because of regulatory reaction to the size of the proposed rate increases. Inflation across the economy was much higher than in the previous decade. Prices increased by 9 percent per annum for all commodities from 1973 to 1981 and by more than that for energy inputs and for the materials important to the production of manufactured goods. Fuel prices increased by almost 22 percent per year, and they prospectively were to be passed through the regulatory process in full at the same time that increased capital and labor costs were being considered the basis for rate increases. Wage rates increased with inflation, but productivity increased only at the reduced rate of 2.4 percent per year.[35] This combination of high factor price increases and low productivity growth brought about sustained increases in operating costs. The companies applied for commensurate price increases, so that there were three times as many new proceedings before the regulatory agencies in the 1970s as in the 1960s (see Appendix A).

Even though many requests were made, and in some part granted, increases in the regulated rates and fares were kept below increases in costs throughout the decade. During the 1973–81 cycle, rates and fares increased on average by 4 to 8 percent per year in the public utility industries and by 7 to 9 percent per year in the transportation industries (as shown in Table 3.6). All of the industries except telephone and telegraph had smaller price increases than necessary to match the

---

[35]*Economic Report of the President* (1978), Tables B-2, B-37, B-55, B-56; and *Economic Report of the President* (1976), Table B-2, (decline from 1973 peak to 1975 trough).

## Table 3.6
### Price Regulated Industries: Average Annual Percentage Change of Implicit Price Deflators

| Industry | 1969–1973 | 1973–1981 | 1981–1987 |
|---|---|---|---|
| Rail transportation | 7.0 | 8.5 | 6.1 |
| *Cost index* | *11.5* | *13.7* | *11.9* |
| Airline passenger service | 6.7 | 7.1 | 6.3 |
| *Cost index* | *6.6* | *8.4* | *4.9* |
| Electric, gas, and sanitary services | 2.4 | 7.7 | 7.0 |
| *Cost index* | *4.0* | *8.7* | *5.0* |
| Telephone and telegraph | 2.5 | 3.8 | 3.9 |
| *Cost index* | *2.2* | *3.9* | *2.4* |

Source: National income and product accounts as updated by the Survey of Current Business (U.S. Department of Commerce) and gross product originating components and net capital stock from bureau of economic analysis (U.S. Department of Commerce).

Computation: As in Table 3.1

cost index increases (given in Table 3.6). The differences per annum were 1.3 percentage points for airlines, 1 percentage point for electric/gas, and 6 percentage points for rail transport. Only telephone and telegraph, with productivity increases that kept cost index increases below the 4 percent level, had been allowed rate increases at the level of cost index increases. On the whole, the regulated sector did worse in price increases necessary to compensate for inflation during the 1970s than other industries.[36]

[36]An alternative comparison is that between industries subject to price regulation and those subject to entry controls but no price controls. There are three entry-controlled industries for which the same series can be compiled—trucking, broadcasting, and banking. Each has been subject to some requirement beyond the licensing conditions. Trucking has been required by the ICC and state agencies to operate subject to cost-plus constraints on sales profit margins. Broadcasting has been required to absorb the costs of public service programs and to meet fairness requirements for the dissemination of alternative political positions. Banking has been subject to limits on the interest rates to be paid to depositors. None of these regula-

These regulatory limits on price increases reduced cash flow in the utility and transportation industries. As shown in Table 3.7, the gross cash flow per dollar of invested capital in these industries fell below levels equivalent to those in unregulated industries elsewhere in the economy. The shortfalls were 4 cents on the dollar of capital in airlines and 3 cents in electricity and gas retailing (given that cash flow per dollar of investment fell 1 to 3 cents below the levels for the comparative industry index). There were no shortfalls for the telephone companies, but the railroads fell 9 cents per dollar behind each year over the nine years of the 1970s cycle.

That the utilities and airlines at least maintained most of their cash flow while prices were being held down was a result of a number of adjustments made in response to regulation. These companies took the opportunity to reorient price

tory practices has been equivalent to the limits on earnings set by agencies practicing rate base − rate of return regulation, so prices could be expected to have increased more rapidly in those industries.

In fact, the experience was as follows:

| Industry | 1969–1973 | 1973–1981 |
|----------|-----------|-----------|
| | (percentage annual average price increase) | |
| Trucking | 3.5  (0.9) | 8.7  (6.7) |
| Broadcasting | 2.6  (2.3) | 6.9  (4.6) |
| Banking | 4.7  (1.8) | 7.3  (4.0) |

Source: As in Table 3.6

The rates of price increase in these industries did not greatly exceed those in the price-controlled industries (in Table 3.6). In fact, all three were lower in the 1969–72 business cycle than any of the price-controlled industries except for telephone services. While trucking had the highest annual rate of price increase in the 1973–81 cycle, broadcasting was second to the lowest (with only telephone services lower).

But the three entry-regulated industries all had price increases through the two high-inflation business cycles that exceeded their cost index estimates (shown in parentheses). While airline and energy company price increases were 1 percentage point lower than cost increases each year in 1973–81, these three entry-controlled industries had price increases 2 to 3 percentage points greater each year than capital and operating cost increases. The regulatory constraints imposed on the energy and communications companies were not binding on price increases in these industries.

**Table 3.7**
Price Regulated Industries: Gross Cash Flow per
Dollar of Net Capital

| Industry | 1969–1973 | 1973–1981 | 1981–1987 |
|---|---|---|---|
| | (annual average, cents per dollar of net capital) | | |
| Rail transportation | 5.5 | 5.1 | 5.4 |
| *Comparative index* | *16.0* | *14.4* | *14.9* |
| Airline passenger service | 12.8 | 12.0 | 11.0 |
| *Comparative index* | *17.6* | *15.8* | *15.8* |
| Electric, gas, and sanitary services | 11.6 | 10.4 | 14.3 |
| *Comparative index* | *14.4* | *13.1* | *14.0* |
| Telephone and telegraph | 14.5 | 12.8 | 13.8 |
| *Comparative index* | *14.7* | *13.3* | *14.2* |

Source: National income and product accounts as updated by the Survey of Current Business (U.S. Department of Commerce) and fixed reproducible wealth table for nonresidential private capital by major industry, current-cost valuation (U.S. Department of Commerce/BEA); market returns calculated from CRSP database.

Computation: As in Table 3.2

structures with, for the most part, the consent of the regulators. They increased the price-level differences between markets where the companies operated under controls and other markets where they sold outside of controls. Prices for services offered in unregulated markets increased more rapidly in the electric, gas, and rail-service industries. In fact, electricity and natural-gas prices in unregulated markets increased at least at twice the rate of those in regulated markets (see Appendix B). Unregulated airline fares on intrastate passenger services in Texas and California were kept more in line with cost changes than were regulated interstate fares, increasing at a 12 percent annual rate by the middle 1970s, while regulated fares were increasing only at a 7 percent rate. To be sure, market conditions rather than regulation could have caused unregulated rates to increase to a greater extent in these industries. But in general the regulated companies kept basic home utility rates down, when inflationary demand and cost conditions otherwise would have caused them to increase, while operating to increase prices rapidly in unregulated, primarily industrial markets.

The second response to regulatory price constraints was to reduce the quality of service. Quality degradation would be difficult to discern with such changes focused on those classes of service where consumers were least likely to react adversely and on those aspects of service least observable. The transportation companies reduced capacity, so that boxcar turn around time increased and the number of serviceable rail boxcars or the number of empty airline passenger seats declined (see Table C). The energy utilities reduced capacity margins, so that when peak demands were realized, delays were encountered or service reductions were more frequent. The reserve margin against natural-gas production fell by one-third between 1969 and 1981, and telephone service delays on days of peak demand increased threefold (as in Table C). Only electric power "improved" service quality as measured in these dimensions, with capacity margin increases of 3.9 percent (but this is a special case: cutbacks in new plant construction were more than matched by reductions in final demands resulting from higher fuel prices).[37]

The new pricing constraint had an impact on the profitability of regulated companies and, consequently, on their investment and on GNP growth. Profitability for investors, as reflected in the stock prices of regulated companies, had already experienced declines relative to that in other companies in the 1969–73 business cycle (included in Table 3.3 and again in Table 3.8). Stockholders' rates of return did not decline further, but instead stayed close to market rates of

[37]Note that the price increases in Table 3.6 do not include fuel, since they are value-added prices net of raw materials costs. Fuel price increases were of the order of the 20 percent per annum registered in the produce price index.

**Table 3.8**

Price Regulated Industries: Stock Market Returns to
Shareholders of Companies in These Industries

| Industry | 1969–1973 | 1973–1981 | 1981–1987 |
|---|---|---|---|
| | (average annual percentage return) | | |
| Railroad transportation | na[a] | na[a] | na[a] |
| *Comparable market return* | na[a] | na[a] | na[a] |
| Airline passenger service | −7.9 | 9.3 | 13.0 |
| *Comparable market return* | *0.9* | *12.2* | *14.9* |
| Electric, gas, and sanitary services | 0.3 | 11.4 | 16.7 |
| *Comparable market return* | *3.4* | *10.1* | *11.9* |
| Telephone and telegraph | 4.3 | 10.8 | 19.9 |
| *Comparable market return* | *3.6* | *9.9* | *12.6* |
| *Value-weighted market-wide return* | 2.7 | 10.7 | 14.5 |

Source: Center for Research in Security Prices (the Graduate School of Business, University of Chicago, CRSP daily stock returns data series).

Computation: As in Table 3.3

[a]Na = not available—see note on Table 3.3.

return in the 1973–81 period—rates on airline shares were 3 percentage points below and on electricity, gas, and telephone shares a percentage point above market profit returns each year (in Table 3.8). The convergence of returns with those generally in the market did not compensate for lower rates of return between 1969 and 1973; indeed, the airlines fell a further 3 points per annum behind in the 1973–81 period, to levels only two-thirds of those in the rest of the market, and the electric and gas companies made up only 10 of the 15 points lost.

Low stockholder returns were not followed by reduced company investment in the 1969–73 cycle, but there were substantial cutbacks in the 1973–81 cycle in these industries. The airline companies undertook investment at the 2 to 3 percent annual rate, half that in the late 1960s and one-fifth of the 15 percent level achieved in the 1960–69 cycle. The railroads continued to reduce their capital stock, in fact by another percentage point per year (and the limited investment that did take place was for equipment for unit trains of coal and other commodities operating under deregulated contract rates). Investment rates in the energy utility industries were reduced to 2 percentage points per annum, less than half those in the previous business cycle (see Table 3.9). Only telephone industry investment, based on rapid and significant technological change, stayed at the 6 percent level achieved in the 1960s. Generally, these rates of investment no longer exceeded those in other industries by the 1 to 2 percentage points realized in earlier business cycles. Although expanding demands for products and services from these companies justified larger outlays for plant and equipment, those outlays except in telephone services were not forthcoming because regulated prices were too low to generate compensatory returns.[38]

[38]The demand and cost conditions consistent with this regulated firm response are shown in Diagram Four. The average total cost curves and demand curves have shifted up from levels 1 to level 2 because of inflation. Price $p_2$ has not been allowed to increase commensurately, so that now $p_2$ is below $ATC_2$. However, the marginal costs are still less than price for additional production. Thus, overall revenues are less than costs ($p_2$ is less than $ATC_2$) while returns at the margin still support GNP growth from $q_1$ to $q_2$ ($p_2$ is greater than $MC$). See Diagram Four below.

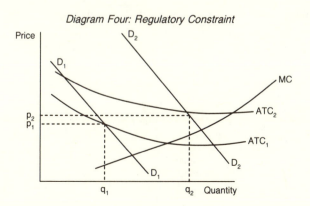

Diagram Four: Regulatory Constraint

But with such sustained lower rates of growth in capital stock, production growth in these industries fell by up to 3 percentage points per annum. Railroad GNP growth, which had been negative for more than a decade, was still negative at $-0.5$ percent per annum. Airline, energy, and telephone service GNP growth rates were positive, but 2 to 3 percentage points lower than in the 1960s. These reductions in GNP growth rates in six of the seven regulated industries, and the continued negative growth rate in the seventh, caused this sector to fall from its leading position in production growth rates (see Table 3.10).

The economic response to regulation is a series of steps. Regulatory constraints on price levels in the 1973–81 cycle in transportation, energy, and communications reduced cash flow below levels comparable to other industries, which in turn reduced investment rates and that kept production from growing at previous high rates. The question is how much reduction in GNP was realized in the 1970s and 1980s as a consequence of this process. That reduction has been estimated using values of two parameters: (1) the investment/cash flow ratio and (2) the GNP/investment ratio for each of the affected industries. There are two steps in the calculation.

**Table 3.9**

Price Regulated Industries: Additions to Net Capital Stock

| Industry | 1969–1973 | 1973–1981 | 1981–1987 |
|---|---|---|---|
| | (percentage annual rate in current dollars) | | |
| Rail transportation | $-1.8$ | $-0.7$ | $-2.2$ |
| Airline passenger service | 4.7 | 2.6 | 1.2 |
| Electric, gas, and sanitary services | 5.0 | 2.4 | 1.8 |
| Telephone and telegraph | 6.6 | 6.0 | 3.7 |
| All other industry | 3.9 | 3.3 | 2.6 |

Source: Net capital stocks (nonresidential, current cost by industry) from fixed reproducible tangible wealth tables (U.S. Department of Commerce/BEA).

## Table 3.10
### Price Regulated Industries: Real GNP Growth Rate

| Industry | 1969–1973 | 1973–1981 | 1981–1987 |
|---|---|---|---|
| | (annual percentage rate) | | |
| Rail transportation | −1.4 | −0.5 | −6.5 |
| Airline passenger service | 4.6 | 2.4 | 3.0 |
| Electric, gas, and sanitary services | 6.3 | 3.6 | 3.1 |
| Telephone and telegraph | 8.6 | 6.6 | 4.6 |
| Gross domestic product less economic regulated industries | 2.7 | 2.3 | 2.9 |

Source: National income and product accounts as updated by the Survey of Current Business (U.S. Department of Commerce).

Computation:

$$\text{Growth rate} = \{(\text{GNP}[\text{year}_{in}]/\text{GNP}[\text{year}_{i-1}])^{1/n}\} - 1,$$

where $n$ = number of years and $i$ = beginning year, in 1982 dollars.

The first step is to multiply loss in cash flow (the comparative index minus actual cash flow per dollar of capital in Table 3.7) by the first parameter, then by investment per dollar of cash flow, to calculate investment shortfall per industry. The second step is to multiply the shortfall by the second parameter, GNP/per dollar of investment, to obtain the estimated loss of gross national product.[39]

For rail transport, this estimated GNP loss was 0.2 percent per annum or 1.8 percent over the 1973–81 business cycle.

[39]With net capital = $K$ and cash flow = $CF$, the first step is to estimate $\beta$ in the equation $\Delta K/K = \alpha + \beta (CF)$ by least squares for each industry with 1960–68 data series. Given the difference of the comparative index cash flow ($CF^*$) and the actual $(CF)$ in Table 3.7 for each industry, the reduction in investment equals $\Delta Kr^*/Kr^* = \beta (CF^* - CF)$ where $\Delta Kr^*/Kr$ denotes that lower level of investment calculated to follow from lower cash flow CF.* Assuming that industry production functions are approximated by Cobb-Douglas, then we determine $B^*(\Delta Kr^*/Kr^*)$ as the estimated lost GNP growth rate where $B$ is the capital share of industry income. For the airline industry the capital stock and cash flow data series were too unstable to generate reliable estimates of $\beta$, so no estimate of GNP losses has been made.

For electric and gas it was 0.5 percent per annum or 4.5 percent over that period. For the telephone and telegraph industries the loss was negligibly different from zero, given that cash flows and thus investment were not reduced by "too low" prices.

Was this the intended result? The response has to be that the choice of the system of control ordained this regulatory result. The control process worked for the regulated companies when costs were falling and prices were constant, as in the 1960s. But when capital and labor costs increased, as they did in the late 1960s and throughout the 1970s, it worked against those companies with prices regulated at historical costs but below current costs.[40] Further, the allowed price increases were too low to match even historical costs. To avoid adverse political responses from groups resisting all rate increases, the agencies simply did not grant price increases in current dollars sufficient to cover cost increases.[41] Thus both

---

[40]Cf. Joskow (1974); Noll (1971), pp. 1,016–32.

[41]The lag of price changes behind cost index changes in electricity and gas had an effect on cash flow in those industries that should be examined in more detail. The price changes and cash flow/capital by year are as follows:

| Year | Electric and Gas Annual Percent Price Changes | Electric and Gas Cash Flow/Net Capital |
|---|---|---|
| 1973 | 4.2  (−5.3) | 11.0  (−2.3) |
| 1974 | 2.8  (−3.0) | 9.2  (−3.7) |
| 1975 | 19.2  (+10.1) | 10.5  (−2.5) |
| 1976 | 12.7  (−1.8) | 10.5  (−2.7) |
| 1977 | 11.3  (−1.3) | 11.1  (−2.2) |
| 1978 | 6.5  (−5.0) | 11.0  (−2.1) |
| 1979 | −0.4  (−11.3) | 9.4  (−3.2) |
| 1980 | 14.1  (+7.8) | 10.2  (−1.6) |
| 1981 | 9.6  (+2.4) | 11.2  (−2.3) |

The excess or shortfall of price changes with respect to cost index changes is shown in parentheses, as is the shortfall of gross cash flow behind that in comparable industries. By 1974, with two years of price change deficiency, the cash shortfall was 3.7 cents per dollar of net capital investment. As price increases caught up with cost

process and goals—particularly that of price stability for its own sake—were at fault in the 1970s.[42]

There were differential impacts of lag and of political factors in the rate proceedings in each industry. The rate increases granted during the 1970s were on average five quarters behind cost changes. In the transportation industries, the allowed increases eventually caught up to cost changes. But in electricity, substantial excesses of cost over price changes were sustained for long periods; and in gas transportation, significant cost excesses also developed when these companies could not pass through to consumers the higher gas wellhead prices allowed under field decontrol that began in the late 1970s. Only in telephone service, where fuel utilization was low and technical change rapid, did price changes keep up with (small) cost changes.[43]

increases, the cash flow deficiency was reduced. But it rose again to 3.2 cents in 1979, after four successive years of price increases lower than cost increases.

[42]The behavior of returns on equity for the Salomon Brothers series of 100 electricity generating companies indicates the role of both factors. The series for 1979 to 1981, the years of most extensive inflation, are as follows:

| Year | Yield on A-Rated Bonds (%) | Allowed Return on Equity (%) | Earned Return on Equity (%) |
|------|------|------|------|
| 1979 | 12.2 | 13.5 | 11.7 |
| 1980 | 15.0 | 14.3 | 11.5 |
| 1981 | 17.1 | 15.3 | 12.8 |

For cost recovery, the electricity generating companies had to be allowed to earn more on outstanding equity than the existing return level on A-rated bonds. But the regulatory agencies only allowed returns 1 to 2 percent lower in 1980 and 1981. These return levels were not earned because of lags in installing and collecting the new rates (as shown by the differences between column two and three, estimated by year). The combination of both rejection of cost-justified rate increases and of lag in implementing increases caused earned equity-returns for the electricity generating companies to be 4 percent below bond interest returns. Cf. Salomon Brothers (1990), p. 3, figure 2.

[43]The impact of the regulatory process is indicated in the annual price changes for the telephone versus the electric/gas industries. The annual price changes and the

Reduced rates of GNP growth in the energy and transportation industries have been a widely noted phenomenon. Many reasons have been offered for this, including new policies against adding to energy and transportation services in order to meet new environmental goals and including the fact that the rates of growth of demand in these infrastructure industries has declined as the domestic economy has matured. Given these reasons, however, lower output growth was probably caused by price and entry regulation. Companies allowed only limited rate increases had become reluctant to initiate new service, were much slower in improving service, and came closer to existing capacity limits when extending service to new customers. These conditions slowed GNP growth in the 1970s in ways that replicated the negative effects of price controls in the natural-gas industry in the late 1960s. In this sense, regulation-induced shortage became the pattern for growth in the regulated industries.

excess/deficiency over cost index changes are as follows (with excess over changes in the cost index in parentheses).

| Year | Telephone and Telegraph | Electric, Gas, and Sanitary |
|------|------------------------|----------------------------|
|      | (Annual % Change)      |                            |
| 1973 | 2.8  (+0.0)            | 4.2   (−5.3)               |
| 1974 | 4.1  (+0.9)            | 2.8   (−3.0)               |
| 1975 | 5.9  (+0.2)            | 19.2  (+10.1)              |
| 1976 | 6.5  (+0.3)            | 12.7  (−1.8)               |
| 1977 | 1.8  (−2.6)            | 11.3  (−1.3)               |
| 1978 | 2.2  (+0.3)            | 6.5   (−5.0)               |
| 1979 | 0.7  (−3.3)            | −0.4  (−11.3)              |
| 1980 | 2.8  (+3.1)            | 14.1  (+7.8)               |
| 1981 | 0.5  (+0.7)            | 9.6   (+2.4)               |

Over the first four years of this business cycle, telephone rates increased by as much as costs and indeed realized an excess of 1.5 percentage points. This was cancelled over the last five years by a succession of shortfalls and recoveries from one year to the next. But electric and gas fell behind in price increases sufficient to recover costs in 1973 and 1974, only to make these up in the excessive price increases during the energy crisis year of 1975. Then these industries fell behind over 1976 through 1979 with a 20 percent price shortfall, which was not made up by the 10 percent excess price increase in 1980 and 1981.

## Conditions after Deregulation in the 1980s

The most recent decade, beginning with recovery from the sharp recession in 1981, brought two fundamental changes to the regulated industries. First, the characteristics of the business cycle were more conducive to investment and GNP growth under price regulation. Second, regulation was eliminated in some of these industries and was reduced in others in reaction to its adverse results of the 1970s.

Coming off the 1970s cycle, characterized by high inflation and low growth, the economy moved to much lower inflation and slightly higher annual rates of GNP increase in the 1980s. Inflation rates were 4.7 percent, down from 9.0 percent, and real GNP growth rates increased from 2.4 to 2.7 percent per annum. As important, the fuel price index declined to 2.3 percent from 21.7 percent per year. With productivity rising from 2.4 percent earlier to 3.2 percent per year, there was less incentive to go to the regulatory agencies for higher prices (indeed, the number of agency case decisions in the 1980s fell to one-quarter of that in the 1970s, as shown in Appendix A).

The second development was more fundamental. With lower service quality and less capacity for growth, the regulated companies faced industrial consumers who had become alienated by the "utility" concept. Rapidly escalating retail prices, due to the more than 20 percent annual increase in fuel costs for both the utilities and transportation companies, added to the perception of home consumers that prices were higher for less reliable and less available service.

In response, Congress phased out the price controls on airlines, trucking companies, railroads, gas producers, and petroleum products companies. Both congressional and agency initiatives led to the development of limited, new markets in which electricity distributing companies could purchase bulk power from new unregulated generating plants. The federal court in accepting the antitrust settlement of the government's case against AT&T brought about the separation of the local telephone operating companies from federal regulation and began the phasing out of federal regulation of long-distance service charges. Thus transportation and energy production were deregulated, while energy distribution and communications at some levels were subject to reductions in regulation.

The results for the transportation and utility industries have been price increases in keeping with cost increases. Annual average price increases have equaled or exceeded the respective cost index changes for all transportation and utility industries except rail transport (see Table 3.6, last column, for the 1981–87 period).[44] These increases generated cash

---

[44]The period of post-regulation has essentially consisted of those years since 1984. That was the second year of full recovery of passenger demands for airline service after the 1981 recession, but the first year of restructuring to a hub-and-spoke system of airline routes. The initial stage of restructuring in telephone services and gas distribution were complete, with substantial de facto deregulation of long-distance (telephone) and field production (gas) services. While there was still much to be done to reduce excess service requirements or redundant capital in rail transport and electricity distribution, these industries as well were in the first phase of deregulation. Their price and cash flow behavior over the period from 1984 to 1987 was strikingly different from that in the previous decade. The series are as follows (with excess of the cost index or comparative index in parentheses):

| | Railroad | | Airline | |
|---|---|---|---|---|
| Year | Price Change | Cash Flow/Capital | Price Change | Cash Flow/Capital |
| 1984 | 5.2 (−5.1) | 6.1 (−9.2) | 1.0 (+3.5) | 12.8 (−3.5) |
| 1985 | 1.1 (−6.7) | 5.7 (−9.7) | −5.8 (−4.4) | 11.2 (−5.2) |
| 1986 | 2.0 (−5.9) | 5.6 (−9.9) | 0.5 (+1.5) | 13.4 (−3.1) |
| 1987 | 1.5 (−8.9) | 5.3 (−10.5) | 7.8 (+5.7) | 19.1 (+2.3) |

| | Telephone | | Electric, Gas, and Sanitary | |
|---|---|---|---|---|
| Year | Price Change | Cash Flow/Capital | Price Change | Cash Flow/Capital |
| 1984 | 5.1 (−1.9) | 13.6 (−1.0) | 5.1 (+4.0) | 15.8 (+1.4) |
| 1985 | 4.4 (+3.3) | 14.7 (+0.0) | 5.4 (−0.2) | 16.0 (+1.5) |
| 1986 | 0.9 (+1.0) | 15.4 (−0.5) | 6.9 (+0.9) | 16.3 (+1.7) |
| 1987 | −4.0 (−1.4) | 15.3 (+0.2) | −0.1 (−4.2) | 15.7 (+1.0) |

The rate of price changes in rail, telephone, and energy industries declined over this period, after increases involving considerable initial recovery of previous cost increases. Only airlines experienced price declines at the time of deregulation, but

flow per dollar of investment capital in excess of index levels for inter-industry parity except for rail and airline services (see Table 3.7) and stock market returns equal to or in excess of those on investment elsewhere in the economy (see Table 3.8; the railroad, airline, electric, gas, and telephone stock returns all were at market levels). Investment growth rates in the utilities were similar but in transportation were still lower than those experienced in other, unregulated industries (as shown in Table 3.9).

With higher relative prices, but the same or lower capacity additions, the GNP growth rates of these industries settled to levels equal to those in the rest of the economy. The exceptions were rail transport, which continued to decline by 6 percent per year in response to declining demand, and telephone services, which as the least deregulated and the least affected by regulation continued to grow 1.7 percent per year more than the all-industry average (see Table 3.10; even so, the rate of growth for the telephone industry GNP was 2 percent below that in the previous, lower-growth business cycle). The other five industries operated as if they were no longer high-growth, low-price industries but instead had become low-growth, higher-price industries similar to those in the manufacturing and trade sectors of the economy. The "utility" experiment was at an end.

**The experience in particular industries: electric power.** Retail prices for electricity were indirectly determined by the state agencies in the process of approving company requests for increased revenues. When faced with sharply increased fuel costs, together with interest rates twice those in the 1960s, the power companies put forward requests to the com-

this industry had the least shortage of capacity. As prices moderated, cash flow increased. Starting at 12 to 15 cents per dollar of capital, cash flow rose to 20 cents per dollar (in all except the railroad industry, which was still declining significantly as late as 1987).

missions for revenue increases of more than 10 percent per year. The number of agency revenue and cost reviews increased, from an average of four per year during the period 1964–68 to 53 in 1972 and 56 in 1973. The time required for a decision consequently increased from roughly eight months to two years, greatly lengthening the interval between request and increased prices. Since the requested increases were based on past cost increases, the consequent delay in case decisions had to cause even the allowed price increases to fall behind then current cost increases.

But more central than process, the content of agency decisions kept price changes below cost changes for the power companies. In cases in 31 states, started in the early 1970s and decided in 1974, the commissions allowed an average rate of return of 8.2 percent (which was 83 percent of that requested by the companies). But prime interest rates, which in 1970 had been 8.8 percent, had risen to 9.7 percent by June 1974. At such a rate of interest, returns for the companies would have been greater if they had ceased using their operating funds and bought government and manufacturing company bonds. In cases involving 100 power companies in 1980, the allowed return was 14.3 percent, the earned return was 11.5 percent, but the yield on A rated bonds was 15 percent.[45] The spread between debt and equity returns was supposed to compensate for the risk of equity investment; with that spread eliminated, equity investment was not attractive at least until the mid-1980s.[46]

As could be expected, capital stringency in electric power became a dominant condition. Further investments based on dollar receipts from new issues to stockholders were out of the question, as electric utility common stock fell in value to about 75 percent of the book value of existing investments.

[45]Cf. Salomon Brothers (1990), p. 3.

[46]MacAvoy and Joskow (1975).

With limited access to equity capital, the power companies issued new debt, but only to the extent allowed by regulatory limits on the debt-equity ratio. As a result, the capacity of plants and equipment to produce electricity did not increase substantially between 1970 and 1985. This long process in which each company cut back on capacity growth had the industry headed towards investment and production short-falls.[47]

An adjustment in the regulatory process prevented short-ages, however, for unintended reasons. A number of the state agencies allowed automatic pass-through of purchased-fuel price increases, so as to reduce the gridlock in the case-by-case decision process. The higher fuel costs, when realized in higher retail prices, resulted in cutbacks in demand. Rather than increasing by 50 percent in ten years as in the 1970s, production increased only by 13 percent in the 1980–87 period, making only limited additions to capacity necessary for expanding production. The very limited expansion allowed by stringent rate controls proved by chance to have been sufficient to meet the limited expansion of demand.

But by the early 1990s, shortages could no longer be post-poned. In early 1990, a leading power-supply forecaster stated that blackouts in the Southeast and in New England were inevitable within the next two years.[48] The core prob-lem according to John Sillin of Management Analysis Com-pany "is that utilities simply aren't building enough new plants . . . (they) don't think State regulators are allowing rate levels that are sufficient to finance new-plant construction."[49] There have been some adjustments in the regulatory process in the face of this condition. To make capacity expansion more attractive, federal statutes have been changed to allow

[47]Ibid.

[48]Cf. *Wall Street Journal* (1990), p. 84.

[49]Ibid.

power distributors to buy electricity from unregulated producers operating cogeneration steam and power plants.[50] This has made it possible to pay wholesale power prices not based on agency rate base/return reviews, but on costs of prospective new capacity. The federal and state agencies have moved this concept forward to allow independent power producers (IPP) still outside of regulation into the transmission grid at unregulated prices and, as IPP power expands to provide more than half of incremental supply, thereby to deregulate the production level of the industry.

**The airline passenger service industry** in the 1980s realized substantial increases in passenger mileage each year from expanded route systems and new feeder systems bringing in through-passengers from remote locations. The elimination of federal entry and fare regulation had much to do with this expansion.

The airlines, in reaction generally to inflation and particularly to the acceleration of fuel costs in the 1970s, had reduced service quality significantly. After increases in investment of 13 percent per year from 1960 to 1969, the domestic airlines cut back capital outlays to 5 percent per annum in the 1969–73 period. This might have been expected, because of the capacity built up in introducing jet service in the earlier expansion. But investment cutbacks, beyond eliminating excess capacity, reduced service-quality levels as well, as shown by a 10 percent decline in the airline-service quality index from 1969 to 1973 and a 6 percent further decline from 1973 to 1977. Throughout this period, as passenger mileage increased, these same passengers were offered less convenient scheduling and more crowded flights.

This state of affairs could very well have extended into the 1980s. Comparisons of projected airframe expansion with

---

[50]Cf. Public Utility Regulatory Policy Act, PL95-117 (1978).

the required level of cash flow to finance that expansion indicated that the regulated airlines did not have access to sufficient financial resources to achieve requisite growth in the new decade.[51] But with deregulation, both established airlines and new entrants increased revenue passenger mileage by 64 percent between 1980 and 1988, by adding 20 percent to plane load factor, 10 percent to the number of seats, and 5 percent to the stage length of each flight. The airlines were allowed to reorganize for higher levels of efficiency, and thus to offer more service at lower rates or fares per passenger mile. Evidence from opening up passenger service markets is still being gathered. Bailey, Graham, and Kaplan[52] found that, while current dollar fares rose, they increased less than average operating costs. Call and Keeler[53] and Morrison and Winston[54] both found that lower profit margins and higher revenue passenger mileage resulted from the outbreak of competition at the end of CAB controls in the early 1980s. But also, fares on high density, long-distance city pair services fell relative to those on local service (Bailey, et al.). Fares on optional travel or on less time-sensitive travel have fallen the most as the airlines have attempted to fill empty seats.

Even so, a rigid price system under regulation has not been replaced with a competitive spot price mechanism for seat space nationwide. Fares for city pair service where there are very few carriers are higher, and reservation systems across airlines foster price collusion and barriers to entry of independent new carriers. Imperfectly competitive city pair markets have replaced imperfect regulatory systems. But the expansion of service to date indicates that gains to consumers

[51]Donaldson, Lufkin, and Jenrette Securities Corporation (1976).

[52]Bailey, Graham, and Kaplan (1985).

[53]Call and Keeler (1985).

[54]Morrison and Winston (1986).

from replacing 1970s regulation with imperfect market competition have been large and consistent over the decade.

**The rail freight service industry** has had some prospect for achieving efficient operations and compensatory revenues after deregulation. The experience with regulation had been with a system of control that curtailed profits, growth of rail capacity, and, ultimately, service in the 1970s. The Interstate Commerce Commission had granted revenue increases almost every year since 1967, but these increases were so limited that, by the end of the 1970s, the industry was earning barely 2 percent on the book value of assets. While declining demand made it less necessary for the railroads to maintain parity in cash flow with other industries, rates of return that low accelerated the liquidation of assets. But the commission was at the same time slow and reluctant to allow abandonment of lines. The railroads had to continue to provide boxcar service for small shippers, on short-distance lines and on small volume but frequent deliveries, even when the direct costs for those services were greater than the revenues from providing them.

To meet service requirements and still earn profits given such regulation, the railroads had to realize monopoly prices on high-volume and long-distance transport services. This distortion of rate structures worked to maintain cash flow only for those roads with a balance between subsidized and high-margin traffic and where the expansion of trucking companies into high-profit margin services could be contained.[55] By the 1980s, trucking and barge lines had succeeded in taking away substantial parts of traffic that was supposed to provide earnings to subsidize low-volume service.

With the passage of the Staggers Act, removing both rate ceilings and service requirements, the major railroads were

[55]Levin (1981), pp. 1–26; and Levin (1977).

able to respond to entry into their high profit-margin markets with reduced rates and to reduce redundant capacity in feeder markets. A consequence of eliminating the control process was the reduction by railroads of costs and margins on high-volume traffic, of track mileage by 20 percent on local service, and (for select traffic including shipments of grain) even of the level of rates. Rates on previously subsidized traffic increased.[56] Rail freight revenues covered direct costs on most services for the first time, so that while they fell across the industry by 20 percent over the period from 1980 to 1988, operating income remained constant or increased. The rail freight industry had begun to recover.

**The telephone industry** experienced only limited adverse effects from regulation. During the 1970s, the state regulators increased the allowed monthly charges for local telephone service by less than the increases in direct costs of that service (or by amounts that at least failed to provide for a greater contribution towards recovery of the joint system costs for providing local and long-distance service). At the same time, the allowed rate increases on long-distance services, while small, were far in excess of increases in costs for those services. The increased profit margins on long-distance service became the source of funds to cover AT&T's joint costs of services in the system. By the middle 1970s, local access and usage charges were two-thirds of the direct costs of providing those services, while long-distance rates were twice the direct costs of those services.[57]

The high and increasing profit margins on long-distance

---

[56]Winston, et al. (1990) estimate that the rate increases resulted in losses to consumers of $1.3 billion, which was more than compensated for by service quality increases worth $4.1 billion. Cf. Table 3.4, p. 28.

[57]Rohlfs (1978). Dr. Rohlfs estimates marginal costs and rates for classes of service in ways that make these order-of-magnitude differences quite likely.

services made a very good case for entry by specialized tele-communications companies into just long-distance markets. That entry had to be allowed by the Federal Communications Commission, even though it would dilute funds to pay for system joint costs, because of a federal court finding that required broad and general certification of new specialized long-distance carriers. At the same time, other revenue sources for AT&T to fund coverage of joint-costs were fore-closed by state regulatory commission limits on basic ex-change rates. AT&T had the responsibility to finance the network, but was losing its funding source in the late 1970s.

This breakdown of the regulatory scheme made the long-run outlook for full service telephone companies similar to that of the energy utility and transportation companies. To be sure, profitability was not being constrained to the point of cutting off investment, as in electric power, because techno-logical improvements had greatly reduced the capital costs required for capacity expansion. But profitability was reduced in high-margin markets, as traffic was diverted to new special-ized competitors and was not allowed to increase in low-margin local markets, given that the state commissions pre-vented any substantial rate increases to home consumers on basic service.

The 1984 divestiture from the Justice Department antitrust proceeding separated long-distance AT&T from the Bell op-erating companies providing local service. At settlement, the divested operating companies filed $11 billion of requests for local rate increases to cover future shortfalls of long-distance subsidies as they left AT&T's internal income-transfer system. Not long after the settlement, the Federal Communications Commission imposed access charges on all local subscribers and reduced interstate long-distance rates by amounts con-sistent with transfer of revenues to the access charges. Local rates with access charges increased at twice the rate of infla-tion, while long-distance rates declined by the rate required by the FCC. But long-distance subsidies did not disappear.

AT&T long-distance continued to pay 60 percent of its operating revenues over to the local companies, not as settlements but as charges for long-distance access to local service. By 1989, five years after divestiture, local rates had increased by 47 percent, while long-distance rates had decreased by only 33 percent, all as given by regulation.

Whether these changes, as forced into the regulatory process by new carrier entry, have benefited the economy is problematical. Shifting the payment of fixed costs onto access charges will reduce subscriber lines on the system to the detriment of all subscribers. Separating AT&T and the operating companies has reduced service convenience, and current requirements on AT&T long-distance rates to include long-distance access charges has reduced investment and GNP growth in the industry (or has shifted it to private systems of large consumers). By the beginning of the new decade there were more companies and a shift of regulations to the state commissions.[58]

## Industry Experience and GNP Growth in the 1980s

The paths towards deregulation in the seven industries were not all the same. The transportation industries were taken out of regulation by federal legislation abolishing controls on interstate services, while the energy utility industries were decontrolled either by Congress or by the federal agencies themselves at the production, but not at the distribution, level. Telecommunications was not decontrolled by the antitrust court but services in long-distance and in local markets were separated and regulation was refocused on local markets. Prices went up by more than costs in all these industries, however, to catch up after previous overly restrictive pricing limits were relaxed. The industries also began to use existing capacity more intensively as service limits were relaxed.

[58]Cf. MacAvoy and Robinson (1985), pp. 225–62.

GNP growth was not at the levels of the 1960s, when the regulated utility concept fostered investment and production increases in the regulated industries one-third to one-half again greater than in the unregulated industries. In fact, GNP growth rates were lower in each of the regulated industries in the 1980s than in the 1970s, predictably because partial deregulation brought about larger relative price increases that, in turn, reduced marginal demands for final consumers. But in all of these industries, GNP growth was not constrained by price controls at supply levels below full demands for service. The $50 billion of losses in GNP incurred by regulation in the 1970s had been eliminated in the 1980s.

# 4
# Health and Safety Regulation

BEGINNING IN THE LATE 1960s, Congress set up a number of regulatory agencies to implement new policy calling for improvement in industrial health and safety, consumer product safety, and the quality of the environment. The reasons for large scale expansion of this type of regulation were numerous and conflicting. But important was increased political awareness of these problem areas and recognition that new regulatory organizations had to substitute for governmental spending programs in dealing with them.

Such well-publicized portents of disaster as Rachel Carson's *Silent Spring* and Ralph Nader's *Unsafe at Any Speed* had enhanced general concern for environmental or industrial health and product safety. The question was how to deal with these problems, and the answer was to be found in the regulatory agency process.

Congress and the state legislatures turned to the regulatory process, not only to avoid new taxes and governmental spending, but also as the more efficient way to make industry safer and cleaner. Agencies could impose costly penalties on producers causing the social harms, which could serve both as an incentive for reduction of pollution and as a way to pay for cleanup. In 1967, it appeared to all concerned that the existing agencies were indeed able to complete detailed case reviews of complex issues and announce decisions that promised enhanced service to consumers. This may have been more perception than reality. But the same kinds of results would have been expected of new agencies about to become expert not only on food safety, but also on harms from air pollution and automobile defects as well.

Even so, the new health and safety agencies were moving into uncharted territory. They were supposed to operate with procedures laid out by Congress quite different from, even antithetical to, those of either the price-control or drug safety agencies. While the new legislation defined general goals in terms of lives saved or better health conditions attained, regulatory compliance was to be achieved by having companies install new control equipment. In contrast with the reasonable conditions called for in statutes being defined as to content in agency case decisions, "healthful" conditions were specified in the statutes directly in terms of plant equipment and operating requirements.

Three agencies were to be the new leaders in this regulatory process, the Environmental Protection Agency (EPA), the National Highway Traffic Safety Administration (NHTSA), and the Occupational Safety and Health Administration (OSHA). Their operations had significant effects on production and trade throughout the economy. As will be explained in the following sections of this chapter, these results have been substantially more adverse to the growth of the economy than those from price regulation.

### The Processes of Health and Safety Regulation

Once established, these three key agencies were locked into procedures to make companies comply with specific requirements already in the statutes for "safe" or "clean" equipment. Perhaps this statute designation was necessary for regulating all the companies in the economy in the same way in the myriads of activities that had effects on health and safety.

But one of the consequences was that agencies moved away from attempting to improve health toward establishing guidelines for certifying types of machines and operating procedures.

This direction in regulation can be found in the performance of the three agencies, from their approaches to improving health and safety as they set up for business in the 1970s to their established practices during the 1980s. Each agency is described here in turn, before being evaluated for the economy-wide effects of their general regulatory approach.

### The Environmental Protection Agency

Although there had been local nuisance laws pertaining to pollution for decades, the Congress set new policy in the 1960s by establishing new laws that would require air-pollution abatement in and across the states (in the amended Clean Air Act, Public Law 88-206 of 1963, and the Air Quality Act, Public Law 90-148 of 1967). The second of two Congressional acts required air-quality standards and limits on emissions of motor vehicles "as soon as practicable, given appropriate consideration to technological feasibility and economic costs." But the new policy was not operational until the Clean Air Act Amendments of 1970 (Public Law 91-604) were passed to "speed up, expand, and intensify the war against air pollution in the United States with a view to assuring that the air we breathe throughout the nation is wholesome once again." To achieve this goal, the Environmental Protection Agency (EPA) was to establish national air-quality standards based on health criteria within a year and to require that each state government produce a State Implementation Plan (SIP) showing the steps to be taken to meet the standards within three years.[59] The new agency was organized as

---

[59]In addition, for the first time Congress set specific product performance standards by stating the maximum allowed emissions of hydrocarbons, carbon monoxide, and other pollutants from automobiles. Deadlines for meeting these standards were

a branch of the executive office to require individual industries to comply with the plans and to set limits on pollution emitted by new plants or by motor vehicles across all the states. For the state responses that followed, the new agency provided another key regulatory input as well. Even though the Clean Air Act was framed in terms of goals for air, water, and land quality, the SIP and compliance with the SIP on the state level had to be judged in more concrete terms. They turned out to be by observing the presence of pollution-control equipment. The EPA accepted the SIP, and recognized factory operations as in-compliance, if specified control equipment was in place. Regulation in effect determined that having equipment was equivalent to making the required improvements in the quality of the environment.

In practice, the equipment standards were substantially the same across plants in an industry, and thus proved insensitive to differences in air quality resulting from unique combinations of emissions from plants at different locations. And, while the regulations were specific to the industry, their application also varied widely among the different states. The various state environmental control agencies granted postponements and waivers based on the adverse impact implementation would have on the company or community. Exceptions were granted to older plants, because of their vulnerable competitive positions, but these were the plants where control equipment would have had the most substantial impact on pollution reduction. Whatever the reasons, delays in the development of the SIP and numerous exceptions and variances in those plans rendered the coverage of

extended in the Clean Air Act Amendments of 1977 (Public Law 95-95), and the process itself was extended with the EPA administrator allowed to use design standards rather than performance standards: "If in the judgment of the administrator it is not feasible to prescribe or enforce a standard of performance he may instead promulgate a design, equipment, work practice or operational standard or combination thereof which reflects the best technological system of continuous emission reduction" (91 STAT. 699).

industry by control equipment requirements less than complete in the 1970s.

## The National Highway Traffic Safety Administration

Automobile safety regulation developed specific equipment standards even further. Policy on highway safety began with the establishment of two agencies in the Department of Commerce in 1966—the National Traffic Safety Agency (under Public Law 89-563) and the National Highway Safety Agency (under Public Law 89-564)—which were combined by executive order in 1967 to form the National Highway Traffic Safety Administration (NHTSA). The purpose of regulation in the 1966 act was "to reduce traffic accidents and deaths and injuries to persons resulting from traffic accidents . . . [by] establish[ing] safety standards for motor vehicles and equipment in interstate commerce and . . . undertake[ing to] support necessary safety research and development." But when Section 102(2) of Public Law 89-563[60] defined standards as "the minimum standard for motor vehicle equipment performance," in practice it required the agency to write specifications for parts, assemblies, and systems in automobiles sold in this country.[61] As these standards were filled out, they became design drawings of steering columns, brake drums, and bumpers that allowed only limited variants on each piece of equipment.[62]

[60]See National Traffic and Motor Vehicle Safety Act (1966), p. 6. Public Law 89-563, September 9, 1966, 80 STAT 718; see Senate Report No. 1301, 89th Congress, 2d Sess., 1966.

[61]One contributing factor was the urgency of meeting a schedule for beginning operations to meet statute requirements. The two original agencies adopted the Government Services Administration's equipment standards for government-purchased vehicles and those of the Society of Automotive Engineers for vehicle safety. Both of these sets of standards were design oriented.

[62]The Senate Report in 1966 required that "every standard be stated in objective terms" within a short time period. See Annual Report of the National Highway Safety Agency (1967), p. 50. The Senate had made it clear, however, at the time of the

*The Occupational Safety and Health Administration*

The regulation of worker safety went the furthest toward specifying equipment as both the means and the ends of the control process. The OSHA Act of 1970 had as its goal to reverse the rising number of worker accidents during the 1960s. When it became law, however, it required the Secretary of Labor to set safety standards by specifying "safe" equipment (and in fact the agency quickly adopted equipment requirements as determined over the previous two decades by voluntary industry health and safety organizations). The resulting standards contained detailed specifications of the physical dimensions of production lines, ranging over descriptions of a clean working area to the shape of mesh screens on moving machinery. For example, ladder standards provided that "the general slope of grain shall not be steeper than 1 in 15 rungs and cleats. For all ladders cross-grain not steeper than 1 in 12 are permitted."[63] But while they were the most detailed equipment requirements yet written, they were not comprehensive. The voluntary standards of the industrial health organizations that were OSHA's sources covered certain types of equipment in detail but did not include other types outside of their organizational jurisdiction. For example, of two dozen types of wood-turning equipment, safeguards for half were described, but the remaining types were not even mentioned.[64] In general, safety regulations were full

passage of the statute that the regulation was to be conducted through the issuance of performance standards rather than design or equipment standards: "Both the interim standards and the new and revised standards are expected to be performance standards, specifying the required minimum safe performance of vehicles but not the manner in which the manufacturer is to achieve the specified performance" (89th Cong., 2d Sess., June 23, 1966, p. 6). This was intended to avoid rigidities created by regulation in the design of equipment and to promote technological advancement. (House Report, 89th Cong., 2d Sess., 1966, p. 15).

[63]U.S. Code of Regulations, Title 29, Section 1910.25(b)(3)(ii).

[64]MacAvoy, ed. (1977).

and complete for some, but nonexistent for other plant conditions.[65]

By 1973 the safety standards most frequently violated were in machine guarding, electrical codes, placement and condition of fire extinguishers, floor and wall openings, walking and working surfaces, and in the use of flammable liquids. But this was because they involved the standards that had been developed in the greatest detail, so that OSHA inspection officers could cite them most often.

The three sets of agency practices indicate that a fairly general system had developed for applying this new type of regulation. Although statutory goals were set out in terms of improving health and safety, the regulatory process consisted

[65]At the same time, health standards were virtually nonexistent. Standard setting to protect health rather than safety had only begun in OSHA's first five years. During the summer of 1973, OSHA issued emergency standards on pesticides and cancer causing chemicals. The first standard protected agricultural workers against the toxic effects of twenty-one pesticides, specifying the time that must elapse before an employee may enter the sprayed area. The second standard protected workers from fourteen carcinogens. Precautions included "(1) prohibiting use of toilet facilities and drinking fountains inside a controlled area; (2) prohibiting smoking, smoking materials, food beverages in controlled areas; (3) posting warning signs, etc." (*Job, Safety and Health,* July 1973, p. 21). In May 1974, OSHA proposed a permanent standard stating that "workers should not be exposed to any detectable level of vinyl chloride, a cancer-causing chemical widely used in the plastics industry" ("New Standard: Vinyl Chloride," *Job, Safety and Health,* July 1974, p. 9). During the fall of 1975 new health standards were introduced to regulate asbestos, toluene, alkyl benzenes, ketones, cyclohexane, and ozone. The exposure limit to asbestos was reduced as was exposure time to toluene. Requirements were set for medical examinations, record keeping, monitoring workplace air, and training employees using toluene. In late 1977, OSHA proposed new standards for more suspected carcinogens in the workplace. Depending on the severity of the findings from data analysis on cancer incidence, OSHA would issue either a temporary emergency order until a permanent standard could be issued or would hold public hearings before standards were set. All of these steps in health regulation have been for the purpose of developing a set of standards comparable in scope and magnitude to those in the consensus set of safety regulations. Since they cover very few substances and their scope is limited to emergency coverage in a number of cases, no detailed and comprehensive assessment of OSHA health regulation can be undertaken at this time.

of enforcing detailed equipment specifications. When applied to the individual plant, they required expenditures but not changes in operations directly increasing safety or reducing health hazards.

Given this system, then, agency operations can scarcely be expected to have had the direct results on safety and health intended by the statutes. In fact, there has been extensive and widespread criticism of the lack of such effects from the operations of the new agencies.

### The Costs of New Regulations

By requiring new equipment across manufacturing industries, the agencies regulating health and safety predictably increased costs. Such outlays and the use of less efficient processes associated with the equipment resulted in higher prices for consumer goods from industries most affected by regulation. This impact on prices during the 1970s constitutes the major cost of regulation.

The outlays for plant and equipment to deal with the EPA, OSHA, and NHTSA requirements were concentrated in a few industries. Pollution-related plant investments for 1975 were $6.6 billion, and five industries—electric utilities, petroleum refining, chemicals, nonferrous metals, and paper—accounted for 70 percent of these expenditures.[66] More to the point, these mandated expenditures accounted for a large share of the total investment outlays in the five industries. For each of these five, and also for the construction materials and steel industries, 10 percent of total net investment that year was devoted to equipment for pollution abatement. For safety-related regulations in conjunction with NHTSA equipment requirements and for pollution control regulation at

---

[66]*Environmental Quality—1976, the Seventh Annual Report of the Council on Environmental Quality* (Washington, DC: U.S. Government Printing Office, 1976), pp. 144–247.

EPA, the automobile companies in 1975 used more than half of their addition to net capital stock.[67] As a result of OSHA regulations, companies throughout the economy spent $4 billion that year.[68] And again, certain industries bore most of these expenses—the chemical, metals, wood, paper, and automobile industries made up more than 40 percent of the total.

The installation of safety and pollution control equipment increased operating costs, resulting immediately in higher prices. In the long run, diversion of investment to satisfy regulatory requirements should have led to lower growth of capacity relative to levels in other industries. In both the short and long runs, the impact of regulation should have been similar to that from specific industry taxes—higher prices and lower production growth rates as compared to industries not subject to the cost of controls.

Price increases in those most affected industries in fact were high during the 1973–81 business cycle. Between 8 and 9 percent in nondurable manufacturing, construction materials, and metals, they reached 13 percent per annum in mining. Only motor vehicles had increases close to 5 percent below those elsewhere in the economy (see Table 4.1). But none of these increases need have been extraordinary in the sense of being greater than would have occurred in the absence of regulation.

In fact, the price increases that would have maintained cash flow parity with other industries were more than the actual increases in nondurable manufacturing, construction materials, and metals (as indicated by estimates for the cost

[67]"Impact of Government Regulations on General Motors," paper provided through private correspondence, August 1977. Cf. Crandall (1986), Table 3-5, costs per vehicle, multiplied by Table 2-2, number of vehicles, as a percent of industry additions to net capital stock.

[68]The McGraw-Hill Publications Company Economics Department, *Fifth Annual McGraw-Hill Survey Investment in Employee Safety and Health* (May 1977).

**Table 4.1**

Health and Safety Regulated Industries: Average Annual
Percentage Change of Implicit Price Deflators

| Industry | 1973–1981 | 1981–1987 |
|---|---|---|
| Metal and coal mining | 13.1 | − 2.2 |
| *Cost index* | *15.1* | *1.3* |
| | (5.8) | (0.0) |
| Stone, glass, and clay and | | |
| primary metal industries | 9.1 | 2.4 |
| *Cost index* | *11.4* | *3.8* |
| | (2.9) | (0.1) |
| Motor vehicles | 5.0 | 6.5 |
| *Cost index* | *11.3* | *5.1* |
| | (5.6) | (3.5) |
| Nondurable manufacturing[a] | 7.9 | 4.8 |
| *Cost index* | *10.9* | *3.0* |
| | (4.2) | (0.9) |

Source: National income and product accounts as updated by the Survey of Current
Business (U.S. Department of Commerce).

Computation: Implicit price deflator is current GNP/constant GNP × 100 in 1982
dollars. The annual growth rate equals $\{(IPD[\text{year}_{i+n}]/IPD[\text{year}_{i-1}])^{1/n}\} - 1$,
where $n$ is number of years and $i$ is beginning year of group. The estimates in
parentheses are percentage changes due to regulatory costs, including return to
capital equipment required by EPA, OSHA, and NHTSA and average of operating
costs for EPA and NHTSA regulations as explained in the text.

[a]Paper and allied products; chemicals and allied products; petroleum and coal
products

index shown in Table 4.1; for the calculation method for
establishing an index for cash flow parity per dollar of capital
investment, see Table 3.1). Actual price changes were 2 percent less than index increases in mining and 2.3 percent less
than index increases in construction materials and metals.
They were 3 percentage points less in nondurable goods manufacturing and 6.3 percentage points less in automobile manufacturing than index changes as well.

Overall, the industries included in the group potentially
most affected by the new regulation experienced large price

increases because cost increases were above the all-industry average and output growth rates were low. But there was another justification for such large increases—the increased operating and capital costs associated with regulatory compliance required more cash flow. The current-year recovery of these costs would have justified price increases as shown in the parentheses in Table 4.1—5 to 6 percent per annum in the mining and automobile industries, 4 percent per annum in nondurable manufacturing, and 3 percent per annum in construction products and primary metals. But prices did not increase sufficiently in any industry, to recover both increases in general operating costs and these new regulatory costs. Since the regulatory costs have been by and large the capital costs for which recovery is price-determined, then not all was recovered (as shown by the difference between the actual price increase and the cost index). In fact, no more than half of the regulatory cost increases were realized in price increases in the mining and nondurables industries, and none of the cost increases were recovered in price increases in the automobile industry. While the case for a greater price increase was there in regulatory costs, the market conditions were not such that the full extent of regulatory price increases could be realized.

Even so, given only the limited increase in prices associated with regulation, GNP growth in these industries was at lower annual rates than earlier and lower than in other industries (see Table 4.2). Growth rates were negative for construction materials, metals, and automobiles. They averaged 2 percent for nondurable manufacturing, which was less than half of that in the two previous business cycles and was 1 percent less than the rate achieved in all other industries. Only mining managed to realize both "high" price and substantial GNP growth at the same time, with the rate of price increase only 2 percent less than increases in the index and with GNP growth matching the all-industry average.[69]

---

[69]Demand increases specific to metals in periods of high inflation explain a substantial part of this behavior. Large increases in the economy-wide price index and in the

## Table 4.2
### Health and Safety Regulated Industries: Annual Growth Rates in Constant Dollar Gross National Product

| Industry | 1973–1981 | 1981–1987 |
|---|---|---|
| | (Percent) | |
| Metal and coal mining | 2.8 | 0.5 |
| Due to regulation | (−0.7) | (0.0) |
| Stone, glass, and clay and primary metal industries | 0.0 | −2.2 |
| Due to regulation | (−0.3) | (0.0) |
| Motor vehicles | −1.3 | 2.5 |
| Due to regulation | (0.0) | (−5.3) [c] |
| Nondurable manufacturing [a] | 2.0 | 3.4 |
| Due to regulation | (−0.3) | (−0.2) [d] |
| Rest of the economy [b] | 2.7 | 3.0 |

Source: National income and product accounts as updated by the survey of current business (U.S. Department of Commerce).

Computation:

$$\text{Growth rate} = \{(IPD[\text{year}_{i+n}]/IPD[\text{year}_{i-1}])^{1/n}\} - 1,$$

where $n$ = number of years and $i$ = beginning year of group. Estimates in parentheses are changes in the growth rate consistent with higher prices from higher regulatory costs in those industries as in Table 4.1, based on $\Delta q/q = (\Delta p/p)e$, where $e$ is an accepted or widely used measure of elasticity of demand.

[a] Paper and allied products; chemicals and allied products; petroleum and coal products

[b] U.S. domestic economy less the industries analyzed

[c] Associated with annual price level increase of 4.9 percent per annum from make up of the regulation-induced cost increases incurred from 1973 to 1981, but not taken in price increases in that period

[d] Associated with 2.7 percent price level increase per annum with make up of the regulatory costs from the previous business cycle as in footnote c

value of the dollar against other currencies add to the demands for metals inventories. These conditions marked the 1973–80 business cycle. See MacAvoy (1990), pp. 1–53.

To be sure, these reduced rates of GNP growth were associated with secular downturns in demand for materials, particularly in construction and durable manufacturing. But they must have been also the result of rising relative costs and prices, in part associated with the new regulation. Metals and coal mining lost more than 0.5 percent in GNP growth per annum, and both construction materials and nondurable manufacturing lost 0.3 percent per annum, due to price increases associated with the new regulation in the 1970s (as shown in parentheses in Table 4.2).

The GNP effects from regulation can also be indicated by the changes in the price and production behavior of the most regulated industries during recent inflationary periods. Table 4.3 shows that the 1980–82 price increases matched or exceeded earlier price increases in the affected industries. But constant dollar GNP changes were much lower than in the earlier periods. The contrast with the two earlier inflationary periods indicates that regulations can generate extended output reductions independent of the general inflationary process.

The five years following the 1981–82 inflation made up a period of renewed economic growth and moderate inflation. At the same time, the Reagan administration held back on putting regulatory requirements in place. Capital outlays on pollution-control equipment peaked in 1979, and operating expenses, while continuing to increase, did so at a lower annual rate. Outlays for compliance with occupational safety also declined as enforcement activities were cut back; and the large expenditures on making a safer automobile required by NHTSA's specifying equipment had been made. All of these changes together constituted a slowdown in the imposition of further costs involved in the new social regulation.

The lessened impact from regulation has been reflected in low rates of price increases. Prices in the most regulated industries could have been expected to increase from 1.3 to 5.2 percent per annum in the 1981–87 business cycle (as

### Table 4.3
#### Performance during Inflationary Periods of Industries Subject to Health and Safety Regulation

| Industry | 1950–1951 | | 1973–1975 | | 1980–1982 | |
|---|---|---|---|---|---|---|
| | Prices | Output | Prices | Output | Prices | Output |
| | (annual average percentage increase) | | | | | |
| Metal and coal mining | 3.3 | 1.2 | 32.3 | − 0.1 | 6.2 | − 2.2 |
| Stone, glass and clay and primary metal | 5.4 | 17.0 | 11.9 | − 1.6 | 4.1 | − 9.4 |
| Motor vehicle | − 0.2 | − 4.7 | 0.1 | − 3.2 | 10.3 | − 14.0 |
| Nondurable manufacturing[a] | 16.5 | 5.8 | 10.3 | − 0.3 | 11.0 | − 1.3 |
| Comparison group[b] | 4.6 | 10.3 | 8.1 | 1.6 | 8.3 | 0.6 |

Source: National income and product accounts (U.S. Department of Commerce, Bureau of Economic Analysis).

[a]Paper and allied products; chemicals and allied products; petroleum and coal products

[b]U.S. domestic economy less the industries analyzed

shown by the cost index in Table 4.1). Actual prices did increase, although by more than required for cash flow parity in automobiles and nondurable manufacturing and less than required in mining and materials. The contributions made to those price increases by regulation-induced cost increases was substantially lower than in the previous business cycle in mining and in durable manufacturing (as shown by the estimates in parentheses in Table 4.1).

Given regulation and a variety of other factors, the GNP growth rates in these industries were low, relative both to previous rates and to current rates in the rest of the economy. They were essentially zero in mining, construction materials, and durables manufacturing, and, while positive in automobiles, were far below historical rates in that industry. Only in nondurables were rates increasing faster than those for the rest of the economy (see Table 4.2). But the reductions in growth rates due to regulatory costs were probably not significant in mining, construction materials, and nondurables, because their prices were evidently not increased by higher regulatory costs. It is more difficult to estimate reductions due to regulation in automobile manufacturing. If domestic markets were not competitive and prices increased over time because of changes in exchange rates either fostering or preventing foreign entry, then regulatory costs were just absorbed in lower margins. But if markets were sufficiently competitive domestically to hold prices to long-run marginal cost levels, then the 1980s price increases were regulatory-cost justified. If these conditions held, the GNP reductions from the complex of regulatory requirements on auto production were as much as 5 percent per annum (as in Table 4.2).

The conclusion is that the outlays on control equipment reduced the growth of GNP in the manufacturing industries. The scale of the reductions was probably between 1 and (at the most) 5 percent per year per industry for a small number of most affected industries. Even so, shifting of capital outlays to purchasing pollution-abatement and occupational safety equipment should not greatly affect future production growth. The trend in rates of growth in the most regulated parts of the economy could return to preregulation levels unless there is a new injection of costs from escalating control requirements.

## The Benefits from Environmental and Safety Regulation

Improved health and safety were supposed to be the benefits to result from the activities of the new regulatory agencies. Pollution and lack of safety in plants were to be eliminated by applying the new controls at EPA, OSHA, and NHTSA. But widespread use of controls in industry has not in fact resulted in a significant improvement in health conditions in the 1970s and 1980s.

This lack of measurable benefits can be explained. The most heavily regulated industries have installed much of the required equipment, if slowly and with important exceptions, so that regulation has produced some response. But the linkage between equipment requirements and health conditions has not been established to the extent required to produce widespread health improvements. Both regulatory technique and implementation were at fault.

### Effects of OSHA Regulation

There have not been significant and widespread reductions in worker accidents due specifically to agency activities. Perhaps not much reduction could have been expected, given OSHA's focus on regulating plant and equipment specifications, rather than on more effective measures such as worker training, incentives for accident avoidance, or penalties for high accident rates. OSHA, as an administrative agency, became concerned with safer equipment in the late 1960s because its statute required that standards be promulgated as soon as it began operations. In an early study of the impact of the state safety agencies enforcing the OSHA equipment standards, Sands found that regulatory activities had had only limited impact on injury rates.[70] This resulted from generally low levels of enforcement (the state agencies spent on average one dollar per year per worker on detecting and enforcing compliance). But more likely, the program was more at fault by focusing on machinery rather than on the systems and personnel that put that machinery into unsafe operations.

According to Smith, even intensive enforcement of safety standards could not reduce accidents in target industries, and DiPietro found that accident rates in companies that had been inspected by OSHA did not differ from rates in companies not inspected (in more than half the cases, higher accident rates could be associated with inspection activities by the agency).[71] These studies, centering on evaluating OSHA's operations, have been complemented by an assessment of state agency enforcement in California that raises the fundamental issue of whether such systems can work. Mendeloff found that lost-workday injury rates were not reduced after regulation began in that state. Focusing on types of injuries identified by safety engineers as most likely to be reduced by the equipment standard regulatory process, Mendeloff used data from the pre-OSHA period to predict what the lost-workday injury rate in certain manufacturing industries

---

[70]Sands (1968), pp. 165–79.

[71]Smith (1976), pp. 87–88, Appendix A; DiPietro (1976). The analysis is based on regression equations for each size group; workday accident incidence rates were explained by previous incidence rates and the occurrence of inspections. The coefficients for the inspection variable were not significantly different from zero, but in certain regressions they were both positive and significant, indicating that the occurrence of OSHA inspections was accompanied by higher accident rates. DiPietro offered explanations for the seemingly perverse results: (1) incorrectly specified lag structures in the regression equations, (2) increased record-keeping in the companies raised the accident rate statistics but not accident rates, (3) higher accident rates encouraged more inspections. While the last is the most plausible, the conclusion still was that there was no evidence that OSHA activity reduced accident rates in these industries in the early 1970s.

would be if there still were no regulation. Actual lost-workday rates were in fact not significantly lower than those predicted, implying that the operations of state safety agencies did not reduce accident rates.[72]

Extensions of these studies to assess industry responses to new safety regulations in the 1980s did produce the first findings of a significant if small impact from safety regulation.[73] As enforcement increased, accident rates were still only marginally reduced because of a weak relationship between accidents and "safe" equipment required for compliance.[74] Substantial expenditures by companies for in-compliance equipment—in the billions of dollars—to pass OSHA inspections did not bring about a reduction in numbers of accidents. The expenditures of thousands of smaller companies had limited accident-reducing effects in working conditions where less attention has been paid to workplace safety.

Throughout the 1980s, OSHA failed to establish a pattern of effective improvements in working conditions. This was probably not because of inadequate compliance, given that as the new agency became established, "Firms normally [would] come into compliance when they replace[d] obsolete ma-

[72]Mendeloff (1976). The author used a regression model to explain the annual changes in the U.S. injury rate as a result of changes in new hire rates, lagged changes in new hire rates, changes in the percentage of male workers in the age group from 18–24, changes in the hourly average earnings of production workers and manufacturing, and a constant term. These factors explained 83 percent of the variation in the annual injury rate during these years, and their net effect was to reduce the injury rate in the 1950s and increase it in the 1960s. Using the regression model to predict injury rate changes for the post-OSHA years, the author finds that the predicted (unregulated) accident rates were higher than actual rates, but well within the prediction error of the model so that the two rates of change were not distinguishable. With respect to the California experience, similar regression analyses of specific injury types showed a decline after regulation but not significantly in most cases; also declines expected to be shown from OSHA's target-industry program occurred only in the lumber industry and only in one year but not in other target industries.

[73]Cooke and Gartski (1981); Smith (1979).

[74]See Bartel and Thomas (1985).

chinery. . . . Manufacturers [would be] unlikely to offer equipment that violates standards.[75] There were not significant improvements in accident rates because equipment safety controls did not play the central role in accident occurrence.

### Effects of NHTSA Regulation

The regulation of safety equipment in automobiles produced similar results. In their early years of operation, the two original federal highway safety agencies directed their activities toward improving crash survivability. They issued twenty-nine vehicle equipment standards and proposed ninety-five more during 1967 and 1968. Their recommendations included requiring cars to be equipped with passive occupant restraint systems, such as inflatable airbags, to increase survivability in crashes for front-seat occupants. Subsequently, NHTSA implemented these regulations and prepared new ones on steering control, seating systems, seat-belt installation and assembly anchorages, the flammability of interior materials, and the strength of windows and bumpers. The goal to be achieved by these regulations was to decrease the fatality rate per 100 million vehicle-miles by one-third—from 5.4 in 1968 to 3.6 in 1980. The NHTSA position in the 1970s was that "reductions in the number of casualties per crash can be substantially attributed to this emphasis on promulgating equipment requirements." Further gains would be possible "if sufficient resources [would be] devoted on a priority basis to activities which assure a high payoff in loss reduction."[76]

---

[75]In one case "the manufacturers of mechanical power presses supported a tough standard on the assumption that many more firms (would) buy new machines rather than modify old ones under tougher standards," Nichols and Zeckhauser (1977), p. 55.

[76]*Second Annual Report on the Administration of the National Traffic and Motor Vehicle Safety Act of 1966 for the Period January 1, 1968 through December 31, 1968* (Washington, DC: U.S. Government Printing Office, 1969, Order No. 91-1:HDOC.110), p. 12. *1969 Report on Activities Under the National Traffic and Motor Vehicle Safety Act*

But by 1975 the NHTSA Annual Report indicated that substantial differences were emerging between goals and actual results. Accident mortality rates were not declining as expected from implementing vehicle safety standards. One reason was that the first round of standards did no more than codify existing practice. The agency acknowledged that "many of the first safety standards were based on the Society of Automotive Engineer's standards already subscribed to by much of the automotive industry. . . . [But] since [then regulation has] developed standards in advance of industry but within the state of the art, such as those on passive restraints." Requiring equipment that was already part of the automobile was not enough to produce significant results from regulation. More basic is the fact that the first set of standards did not directly address safety and "tended to specify the type of the design, such as the type of glazing to be used in windows [rather than] state performance specifications which manufacturers must meet."

NHTSA still considered regulation responsible for reductions in traffic fatality rates in the early 1970s. The agency stated in 1975 that "the traffic fatality rate has gone down 35.3 percent since inauguration of [its] safety drive in 1967, and 16 percent since 1973. . . . Though assessment of benefits is not possible program-by-program, the cumulative effect of the combination of programs is undeniable." But a major factor in reduction in fatality levels at that time was speed reduction associated with the 55 MPH limit and with higher fuel prices. As NHTSA itself indicated, "While the country experienced reductions in overall highway travel in 1974 of approximately 2.6 percent, the reduction in the number of total accidents was about 5 percent and [in] the number of fatalities was about 17 percent . . . [these being] safety benefits derived from the establishment of the 55 MPH limit."[77]

(Washington, DC: U.S. Government Printing Office, 1970, Order No. TD8 12:969, pp. 9–10).

[77]U.S. National Highway Traffic and Safety Administration (1976), pp. 7, 10–11.

Highway fatality rates depended on many factors, including technological trends, energy prices, speed limits, and regulation of driving equipment. During the remainder of the 1980s these other factors deserved much more credit for further improvement in fatality and injury rates on the highway. Both fatalities and injuries per vehicle mile were determined by driver age, alcohol levels, and income levels, as well as by highway conditions and driving speed.[78] Studies of fatalities throughout the first full decade after mandatory safety devices were implemented concluded that regulation had no specific effect once account was taken of other determinants. Most interesting, lower birth rates before 1950 had resulted in fewer young drivers in the 1970s responsible for the most dangerous driving. At the same time, drivers acted as if they sought to reduce accident and fatality rates, without regard to the required safety equipment, when they had more economically at stake in an accident in terms of lost income and litigation settlements.

Even so, investigation of comparative pre- and postregulation rates undertaken by the General Accounting Office, using samples of more than two million automobiles involved in accidents,[79] found that from 15 to 25 percent fewer deaths and serious injuries to drivers occurred in the 1966–68 model year, automobiles first subject to safety regulation.

There have, however, probably been limited reductions in driver death and injury rates in more recent models due to more extensive regulation. Engineering estimates indicate that crash protection devices required by NHTSA should have reduced fatal or serious injuries by 10 to 20 percent in various

---

[78]Peltzman, *Regulation and Automobile Safety* (1975); Manne and Miller, eds. (1976); and Peltzman, *Journal of Political Economy* (1975), pp. 677–725.

[79]U.S. Comptroller General (1976). The main difference in approach between the Peltzman and GAO studies was that the latter was able to specify and differentiate pre- and postregulation automobile model years and to use these differences to explain changes in mortality rates. But the comptroller's study failed to take account of demographic factors that were important in Peltzman's analysis for producing findings on agency effectiveness.

types of two car accidents, but these reductions have not been verified.[80] The lap-shoulder seat belt that was in part NHTSA-initiated should have reduced fatalities by 30 percent or more in front-end and roll-over crashes, but seat belts have been used by only a minority of drivers and occupants.

The studies of NHTSA operations over two decades do not indicate that agency operations reduced fatalities from automobile accidents. Equipment regulation has probably not benefited the consumer by enough to allow costs to be matched against benefits and considered as changes in GNP as in other industries.

### The Effects of EPA Regulation

The benefits of EPA regulation have not been more extensive than those from operations in the other two agencies. Although there have been results, they have been important only at certain locations and in specific industries.[81] Where the state environmental protection agencies put equipment requirements in place for companies at specific locations as part of the state plans, the EPA in effect had obtained compliance.

Certain air corridors were cleaner than they were five years earlier. In its *Annual Report for 1977,* the Council on Environmental Quality (CEQ) reported that "from 1967 to 1976 hydrocarbon emissions in the San Francisco area were reduced 25 percent and daily observed oxidant levels also declined 25 percent." Carbon monoxide levels in New York City fell: "Although New York's carbon monoxide problem is still severe, projections based on correlated data show greater improvement than anticipated." But the report on Los Angeles was not as encouraging: "Its special geography, climate

---

[80]Crandall et al., (1986), pp. 51–55.

[81]The concern here is with the pollutants having adverse health effects, such as the sulfur and nitrogen oxides or particulates. This, then, excludes discussion of regulations of automotive emissions, which, while much more effective, do not relate to adverse health conditions. Cf. Lawrence A. White (1982).

and dependence on cars may prevent Los Angeles from achieving the oxidant standard" (U.S. Government Printing Office (1977), p. 180).

There were improvements as well in the middle 1970s in water quality in certain waterways, as measured by reduced waste loads and bacterial content. The CEQ found that, based on detailed and comprehensive monitoring of twelve rivers across the country, five rivers showed "significant overall improvement in fecal coliform violation rates: The Willamette, the Colorado, the Red River, the Ohio and the Tennessee Rivers." In particular, "water quality in the Willamette has dramatically improved during the previous decade and even though it has continued sanitary problems, they are mostly related to runoff sewer overflows during high flow periods."[82] Still, total pollutant content fell in the 1970s for only two of the six major air pollutants (particulates and carbon monoxide), while it was constant or increasing for others.[83]

Even though standards have now been enforced for fifteen years, neither the EPA nor the state plans can take the credit for these improvements in nationwide air and water quality. Implementation was too incomplete. Both EPA and CEQ found that plant standards had resulted in new emissions-control equipment in only about one-third of the area in the nation's air-quality regions. At the same time, process improvements from newer technologies, which reduced pollution, were taking place regardless of regulation. Indeed, they were accelerated by the increases in energy prices in 1974 and again in the early 1980s.

---

[82]U.S. Council on Environmental Quality (1976), p. 272. For a number of years, severe dissolved oxygen (DO) depletion during the summer had been a problem in the Willamette River, to the point of causing the river to take on the characteristics of a running sewer. In the middle 1970s, summer DO increased to levels comparable to those in unpolluted waters, as a result of secondary treatment of all point source wastes and of stream-flow augmentation from expanded storage reservoirs. See U.S. Geographic Survey Circular (1977).

[83]U.S. Environmental Protection Agency (1976).

Another important cause for emissions reductions from one year to the next has been the business cycle. The economy-wide demand for goods increased during the middle of the last two decades and then declined at the end of these decades. So has pollution load, as attenuated by the introduction of new technologies and the changing of plant locations.

This complex process of generating stack emissions can be traced through the experience with EPA regulation of manufacturing-plant pollution discharges. From 1973 to 1983, with the SIP process more or less fully in place, emissions of the major air pollutants derived from manufacturing declined. Particulates decreased the most and nitrogen oxides the least. But these declines continued to bear the same relationship to the rate of growth of industrial production as in previous decades. Particulates increased at a rate 6 to 7 points lower and sulfur oxides increased at a rate 5 points lower than the rates of growth of industrial production, just as before the advent of this EPA system of controls (as shown in Table 4.4). Thus lower national emission levels do not show that regulation has been effective.[84]

Further, there were significant changes in emissions from industry to industry throughout the 1970s that cannot be explained by regulation. As regulation was getting underway in the middle 1970s, sulfur oxide emissions from chemical plants were being reduced, but those from petroleum and electric power plants held constant and from mineral products facilities increased. Nitrogen oxide emissions declined in chemicals, metals, and in fuel combustion in commercial and industrial facilities, but increased in electric utilities, mineral

---

[84]Earlier versions of this table also contained percent changes for volatile organic compounds and carbon monoxide. Cf. University of Rochester CRGBP working paper, pp. 83–87. Since volatile organic compounds (VOC) and carbon monoxide (CO) were the results in great part of highway use of automobiles, they have been deleted to meet space constraints on this discussion of regulation of plant and factory emissions. Cf. Office of Air Quality Planners and Standards, U.S. Environmental Protection Agency (1978).

## Table 4.4
### Pollutants Emissions,[a] 1948–1983

| Years[b] | PM[c] | SOX[d] | NOX[e] | Industrial Activity[f] |
|---|---|---|---|---|
| | (annual percent change) | | | |
| 1948–1960[g] | − 2.03 | − 0.85 | 2.58 | 4.05 |
| 1960–1969 | − 1.48 | 3.50 | 3.53 | 5.00 |
| 1969–1973 | − 8.26 | 0.59 | 3.73 | 6.39 |
| 1973–1979 | − 7.34 | − 2.60 | 0.73 | 2.72 |
| 1979–1981 | − 6.46 | − 4.60 | − 1.43 | − 0.49 |
| 1981–1983 | − 5.34 | − 3.42 | − 2.72 | − 1.10 |

Source: U.S. EPA, Office of Air, Noise, and Radiation, Office of Air Quality Planning and Standards, *National Air Pollutant Emission Estimates*, 1940–1983, EPA 450/4-89-028, (December, 1984): 2.

Computation: All percentages calculated as $[(y_1/y_t)^{1/t} - 1]$ for a period of $t$ years.

[a]Emissions measured in teragrams per year; includes emissions from both stationary and mobile sources.

[b]Years chosen are National Bureau of Economic Research business cycle peaks except for 1960, which is a year after the 1959 peak. Data for 1959 pollutant levels are not available.

[c]PM   = Particulate matter

[d]SOX  = Sulfur oxides

[e]NOX  = Nitrogen oxides

[f]1948 emission estimates are interpolated from 1940 and 1950 emission estimates based on rates of coal consumption.

[g]Industrial production index from *Economic Report of the President*, (March 1984).

products, and petroleum refining.[85] Particulate emissions declined in chemicals, metals, and mineral products, but increased in petroleum refining. Application of the SIPs could not have been effective in controlling emissions.

The reductions actually realized should have resulted in improvements in air quality. To be sure, it is not likely that such improvements would have taken place immediately,

[85]U.S. Environmental Protection Agency, Office of Air Quality Planning and Standards, *Annual Assessment of Air Pollution*, (various years).

since uncontrolled emissions from natural sources also have substantial and varying effects on air content. But during the 1970s air quality was improving at a slower rate than before regulation got under way. Sulfur content decreased by 15 percent, but particulate content decreased by only 7 percent between 1973 and 1979, and nitrogen content increased by 12 percent over the same period.[86] These rates were all lower than the 20 percent reductions realized in the 1960s.

Moreover, the timing of the changes in air quality that did take place cannot be associated with implementation of the EPA plant and factory equipment requirements. The SIP requirements were more or less uniform across the country, since they were based on the EPA's specification of available control technology in each industry. But particulate content of the air decreased more in the Northeast and South, where initial content was already lower, than in other parts of the country (see Table 4.5). The sulfur content of the air either increased by the same amount across all four regions of the country (on the one-hour tests, as shown in Table 4.5) or decreased in the Northeast and Northwest, while increasing in the Southeast (according to the annual averages).[87]

Nor did measured air quality achieve the standards set under the 1970 Clean Air Act. More than one-half of the country's major urban areas either just achieved or were in excess of the required air quality levels in sulfur content, with most showing no substantial reduction in levels over the last half of the decade.[88] The nitrogen oxide content of the air in 1979 was so high that 40 of the 45 major urban areas were either at the limit or failing the standard.[89]

Given these various aspects of emissions and air quality, did

[86]Ibid.

[87]U.S. Environmental Protection Agency (1980) and U.S. Environmental Protection Agency (1974).

[88]Cf. U.S. Environmental Protection Agency (1981) pp. 2–8.

[89]Ibid., pp. 2–14.

**Table 4.5**

Comparison of Air Quality Measures, 1972 and 1979

| Region | 1972 | | 1979 | |
| | Mean Ambient Content Level[a] | Number of Air Quality Control Regions | Mean Ambient Content Level[a] | Number of Air Quality Control Regions |
| --- | --- | --- | --- | --- |
| | (micrograms/cu m) | | (micrograms/cu m) | |
| PM: arithmetic mean; 24-hour tests | | | | |
| Midwest[b] | 77.1 | 76 | 70.7 | 105 |
| West[c] | 85.3 | 24 | 77.8 | 34 |
| Northeast[d] | 70.1 | 53 | 54.9 | 55 |
| South[e] | 73.7 | 71 | 57.2 | 84 |
| SOX: arithmetic mean; 1-hour tests | | | | |
| Midwest[b] | 19.5 | 41 | 30.2 | 30 |
| West[c] | 11.7 | 8 | 22.4 | 13 |
| Northeast[d] | 22.5 | 38 | 34.2 | 32 |
| South[e] | 11.9 | 49 | 23.4 | 11 |

Sources: U.S. EPA, Office of Air, Noise, and Radiation, Office of Air Quality Planning and Standards, *Air Quality Data—1979 Annual Statistics,* EPA 450-4-80-014, (September 1980). U.S. EPA, Office of Air, Noise, and Radiation, Office of Air Quality Planning and Standards, *Air Quality Data—1972 Annual Statistics,* EPA 450-2-74-001, (March 1974).

[a]Weighted average of observations from monitoring sites in each region    These numbers are indicators of air quality calculated for purposes of comparison, although not used by EPA as determinants for attainment.

[b]Midwest    = EPA Regions 5, 7, 8

[c]West    = EPA Regions 9, 10

[d]Northeast = EPA Regions 1, 2, 3

[e]South    = EPA Regions 4, 6

EPA regulation by itself have any impact on emissions and by such constraints on emissions have an effect on air quality? The answer requires quantitative analysis. Regression analyses indicate that the major determinants of particulate and sulfur emissions by industry in the 1970s were investment and coal usage rates.[90] Neither factor had a direct relationship with EPA regulation. There are more disquieting indications to the effect that EPA regulation had no impact on pollution discharge levels. These levels turned out to be positively related to expenditures on air pollution control equipment, rather than negatively related to such expenditures, as would be expected if the SIP reduced emissions by requiring the installation of equipment. But in the main, the factors determining changes in emissions from manufacturing plants were economic and not regulatory. Investment in pollution control

---

[90]The relationship between manufacturing and emissions can be characterized by a production function: $Q = f(x_i, e)$ for goods production $Q$ and emissions $e$, based on input factors $x_i$, including labor, materials, and capital. The level of utilization of each input factor $x_i = f(x_j, p_i, P)$ is chosen so that the factor price $p_i$ is equal to the value of marginal product as determined by quantities of other inputs $x_j$ and output price $P$. Pollutant emissions $e$ can also be considered a variable in the production function, because they too incur costs as required by regulation. That is, each company sets emissions so as to make its costs of containing pollutant discharge equal at the margin to the value of goods and services made possible by the additional discharge. These propositions have been formulated for testing at the industry level so that emissions (QEMIT) depend on industry plant and equipment investment (INVEST), fuel usage (COALTON), output price (PRIC), and the level of disposal costs (RCOST). Altogether these economic factors can be said to have an impact on emissions—investment (INVEST), coal utilization (COALTON), and output price (PRIC). At the same time, pollution control policies should reduce emissions by increasing disposal costs (RCOST). The EPA regulatory processes enter into the industry-level determinants of emissions by setting RCOST in the 1970s.

The relationships fitted with data for the period 1973–80 are described in detail in MacAvoy (1986). In general, QEMIT increased as regulation-determined pollution equipment outlays (RCOST) increased. This finding for both particulates and sulfur oxide emissions is the opposite of what has been predicted to result from effective regulation.

The most striking pattern of economic and regulatory effects is found in the fitted equations for nitrogen oxides emissions. The equation coefficients indicated that fuel usage and product price were significant positive determinants of year-to-year nitrogen emissions but that investment was an insignificant determinant. Regulatory determinants as measured by effluent control equipment expenditures also had a positive but insignificant effect on emissions. Altogether, changes in NOX emissions appear to have been the result of fuel usage, as expected, but not of investment in either direct production equipment or regulation-related pollution control equipment.

equipment related to regulation had little effect on emissions levels at the industry level.

The lack of regulatory impact can be explained in two different ways: The new regulatory process of the 1970s was not sufficiently complete to have an impact, and even where installed, this process was characterized by malfunctions that prevented any direct results.

Whether the fault was with the lack of a process or with the regulatory process itself can be determined by comparing the emissions at locations where firms were in SIP compliance with those at other locations where compliance had not yet been established.[91] With respect to sulfur oxide emissions, based on a 1979 sample for six industries in 50 states, there was no difference in the level of emissions of plants in states in compliance and those of plants in states not in compliance. There was more effect from compliance with respect to particulate emissions, since the average level of emissions from plants in states in compliance was significantly lower with respect to nitrogen oxide emissions, plants in in-compliance states had discharge levels similar to plants elsewhere.

But the size of plant coming under the process of regulation seems to count. For particulate emissions, being in compliance reduced emissions in large plants but not in small plants. Any reduction in overall emissions was at least partially cancelled out by the lack of regulatory impact on emissions rates in the numerous small plants found both in the in-compliance and out-of-compliance states. Only in states

---

[91]Emissions estimates used in this analysis were obtained from the National Emissions Data System (NEDS) of the EPA. In this source, emissions caused by manufacturing are aggregated on three levels: the air quality control region, the state, and the nation. It is important to note that the national levels of emissions shown in this report may not be the same as those given in the Trends report underlying the previous set of regressions. The NEDS report includes only those larger point sources, which emit more than 100 tons per year of any one pollutant, and show measured emissions. The Trends report includes all sources in its estimates, but shows calculated emissions.

where there were large plants with high fuel utilization rates and high but newly constrained emissions rates were there effects from SIP regulation. Because of the mix of small and large plants in both in-compliance and out-of-compliance states, there can be no linkage between the implementation of regulations and regional air quality.

### Benefits and GNP Growth

Although the new agencies from time to time claimed that their actions had improved conditions, there were probably only limited gains towards health and safety goals from regulation in the 1970s and 1980s. There may be positive results forthcoming after these agencies have been in operation for another decade. But there may not be, given that those practices and procedures now fully established and in place do not by their nature generate results.

Thus, an assessment of the health and safety regulatory system does not lead to estimates of positive effects on GNP. Safer products, consequent upon regulation, would have been recognized in final markets as better products, so that GNP should have increased. OSHA regulation, by reducing accidents and improving in-plant health conditions, should have increased productivity, resulting in increased production and sales. But the search for OSHA effects has found no direct impact on accident rates and, thus, no measurable GNP effects of these kinds. NHTSA regulation should have made for greater survivability in accidents for automobile occupants. If such effects had been substantial and prolonged, then automobile sales should have been increased. But during the period of concentrated application of NHTSA equipment requirements, automobile price increases fell short of levels required even to cover the increases in cost from regulation, and constant dollar sales growth was negative. EPA regulation, to add to GNP, should have added to the quality of the environment and thereby enhanced the GNP-measured value of recreation and other consumer activities. But we have not been able to determine even the realization of improved environmental quality from this regulation, because there has not been any observable linkage between equipment standards, emissions, and environmental quality.

Altogether these regulatory agencies have increased costs, but they have not brought about the commensurate benefits intended in their enabling legislation. The agencies increased prices to consumers without improving the safety and cleanliness of production. Across the eight most regulated industries, constant dollar GNP was reduced each year by 0.3 percent in the 1973–81 business cycle and by 1.1 percent in the 1980s in each year that regulation has been operating.[92]

[92]These percentages are estimated from the GNP weighted average of the industry-by-industry reductions in Table 4.2.

# 5
# Regulatory Reform

In THE 1970s, government regulation reached its zenith in the establishment of policies on pollution and safety, in the setting of energy, transportation, and communications prices, and in the determination of safe quality in manufactured products. At that point, almost all corporations were affected by some form of regulation, and a quarter of private sector GNP was closely regulated.

But during the inflation-prone business cycles of that decade, price regulation restricted growth to such an extent that GNP was reduced by one-half to 4 percentage points each year per regulated industry. Most of the public utility and common-carrier transportation industries failed to extend service to new communities or to new customers at quality levels comparable to those in the 1960s.

GNP growth was also reduced by health, safety, and environmental regulation. The new controls substantially increased the costs of providing certain manufactured goods, and the higher costs were passed on to consumers in higher prices that reduced demand and, ultimately, sectoral GNP growth. Of course, this regulation was supposed to improve the environment, health, and safety so that there would be compensating increases in GNP in other parts of the economy. But, while there were benefits in some cases, on the whole measurable improvements in safety or in the quality of the environment did not result from the operations of the new agencies.

With substantial costs and limited benefits, GNP growth in the affected industries was reduced by up to 8 percent in the 1980s. In dollar terms, the maximum estimated loss came to more than $50 billion in the 1973–80 period and to that amount once again, plus $78 billion more, in the 1980–87 period (as shown by industry in Table 5.1). The minimum loss would not include that for regulation of the content in automobiles in the 1980s, since that industry's costs arguably were not passed on in price increases, so that the decade's losses would come to the carry over of $50 billion plus new reductions in growth in nondurable manufacturing of $9 billion. Estimating the total effects on GNP from regulatory policies and practices is clearly not simply a matter of adding up the sectoral losses. Intersectoral dependencies of factor costs and demands cause a ripple effect in which losses by sector are passed on as higher input costs elsewhere, resulting

**Table 5.1**
Incremental Reductions in GNP Due to Regulation

| Regulated Industry | 1973–1981 | 1981–1987 |
|---|---|---|
| | ($billion) | |
| Rail transportation | 2.4 | — |
| Airline passenger service | — | — |
| Electric, gas, and sanitary services | 18.0 | — |
| Telephone and telegraph | — | — |
| Metal and coal mining | 5.2 | — |
| Stone, glass, and clay and primary metal industries | 9.4 | — |
| Motor vehicles | — | 68.6 |
| Nondurable manufacturing | 14.6 | 8.7 |
| Total | 49.7 | 78.2 |

Source: Calculated from percentage reductions in GNP growth rates (as estimated in chapters three and four) multiplied by initial year constant dollar gross national product.

in further reductions in output in those less regulated sectors. These primary and secondary effects can only be estimated together by recourse to a general equilibrium model of domestic production and prices. The model utilized for this analysis is the MPS/GE framework developed by Thomas Rutherford, which accepts an input/output matrix of the economy as an existing equilibrium and then removes the constraints used to specify regulations to solve for prices and quantities that would exist in unregulated equilibrium. Various versions of this model, using a wide range of elasticities of substitution for inputs and consumption goods, yielded economy-wide annual losses of 1.5% to 2.0% of GNP per annum when the constraints inherent in regulation bore effects similar to those described here.

These adverse results were not in the strategic designs of the policy makers. But they have been the product of the regulatory process as adopted and refined by those agencies implementing policy. To improve on this performance the price-control systems would have to respond more flexibly to changes in cost and demand in high inflation business cycles. This would require new means for assessing the agencies' performance, no longer giving them high marks for keeping prices constant over long periods of time. Regulation of health, safety, and environmental quality would have to refocus on performance as well, in terms of "bads" reduction rather than in terms of setting equipment specifications and standards.

But would such changes succeed in restoring reliance on regulation? The answer requires an evaluation of the extent of regulatory reform already underway.

### Reform of Price Regulation

The regulatory process was put under pressure in the 1980s, in day-to-day case hearings, in appeals of agency decisions to the courts, and in the legislatures at both the state and federal levels. In response, there was considerable change in administrative practice. New rules accelerated the flow of case decisions, and new standards were established instead of case decisions that in effect did away with political limits on price increases established by "fair return on fair value" procedures. Deregulation was carried through to completion in interstate rail and truck transportation, domestic airline passenger service, and oil and gas wellhead production, as well as in petroleum products.

Where regulation stayed in place, at the state level, the means for effecting change was by relaxing the overly stringent "fair return" standards for price levels. The agencies took two steps: (1) Before a case was decided, temporary rate increases were allowed, and (2) in the case decisions, specific rates on services began to be approved based on the marginal costs for those services. As early as 1977, when electricity rate decisions still took months longer than they had ten years earlier, new temporary rate increases had the effect of bringing rates more in line with current costs. Not only did agencies reduce lag times, but they also allowed larger rate increases as related to current cost increases. The politics had shifted in that direction. Large rate increases encouraged conservation of energy resources. For the electricity generating companies, commission decisions under the Public Utility and Regulation Policy Act after 1978 even allowed higher seasonal and peak demand period rates to limit growth.[93] By 1990, the agencies in twelve states, including those in New York and California, required the use of estimates of marginal costs for rate setting on important classes of electric and gas service. Prices set equal to marginal costs were above average costs for those services, so that marginal cost prices were higher than those that would have been allowed under the established "fair return" procedure.[94] It was possible for

[93]Weiss (1981).

[94]Again, the justification for this was a desire to reduce wastage of resources at the margin. As a matter of course in case decisions, prices were not set at marginal costs,

the revenues from services on which prices were set according to marginal costs to exceed those from prices in the tariff limited by fair return on the rate base.

Such adjustments were not all that was done to make regulation more responsive. The regulatory process was rolled back by moving activities outside the jurisdiction of the commissions. Production of gas and electricity began to take place outside of regulation in new spot markets for gas at the wellhead and in new long-term contract markets for power to be generated by independent companies not subject to price ceilings. Congress and the Federal Energy Regulatory Commission (FERC) fostered these developments by requiring gas pipelines and power transmission systems, as common carriers, to take unregulated wholesale gas and electric energy, and FERC went further by requiring that the gas lines develop transportation agreements rather than deliver their own gas to these final distributors.[95] In effect, the production and delivery at wholesale of public utility services were decontrolled by giving retailers the opportunity to buy their own in national markets and then contract for delivery.

The slicing out of unregulated levels in an industry was carried further in transportation. Congress mandated decontrol of railroad rates, airline passenger fares, and trucking rates in the late 1970s. The changes in industry performance brought about in the last few years by these congressional actions were fundamental. Railroad rate decontrol applied to all service markets except those in which a few railroads were dominant.[96] Airline deregulation phased out controls of pas-

but were set higher on those classes of service for which marginal costs were higher. Cf. National Association of Regulatory Utility Commissioners (1988), Table 106, "Determination of the Cost of Service."

[95]Pierce (1989). Pierce goes further, proposing open access to power transmission capacity in order to promote development of a separate power generation industry outside of regulation.

[96]The federal court of appeals defined a lack of dominance to permit unregulated rate setting in markets where there were at least two competing railroads. See

senger fares over five years, allowing individual carrier fare reductions of up to 50 percent per year, while limiting increases to 5 percent per year beyond inflation on competitive routes.

Even more basic was congressional deregulation of oil and gas production. Gas deregulation took place in stages, by type of producing field, with old fields remaining longer under controls than new fields through a complex sequence of price increases. Oil decontrol followed the same pattern, but moved much more quickly in the first year of the Reagan administration.

We review two of these experiments in decontrol in detail to show how they have affected industry performance.

## Deregulation in Two Industries

The important first steps in phasing out regulation of airline passenger fares and natural-gas field sales were taken by the agencies. Both industries had been under stringent price controls, and, consequently, were having difficulties in generating cash flow for investment in the high inflation business cycles of 1969–73 and 1973–81. The two agencies involved, the Civil Aeronautics Board (CAB) and the Federal Power Commission (later FERC), had already determined by 1975 that their methods of regulation were unduly restrictive. Their guidelines for setting costs of service were too backward looking to permit price adjustments to match actual cost increases in the late 1970s. Moreover, the monopoly and instability rationales for public interest regulation were no longer invoked as they had been by the legislature forty years earlier.

*Commonwealth Edison Company v ICC,* U.S. Court of Appeals (1989), District of Columbia 76-2070.

*Airlines*

In the words of the CAB Chairman John Robson, the problem was not market but regulatory failure: "Because of regulatory inefficiencies neither the airline investor nor the consumer has fully reaped the potential benefits of the industry's enormous past productivity gains and growth."[97] Under Robson and A. E. Kahn, the CAB in the last half of the 1970s abandoned orthodox regulation by suspending scheduling and entry restrictions, and by allowing fare flexibility in city pairs with competing carriers. By the time that the Airline Deregulation Act was passed, controls in the agency had been effectively abolished from within. Decontrol from within had provided enough experimentation with the open market process to establish that service would improve, so that congressmen voting for elimination of the CAB would not later be blamed for market instability, monopoly, or whatever.

Prior to deregulation, the CAB awarded routes sparingly, after reviewing applications on a case-by-case basis. Decisions were based on the relative financial strength of the candidates, with lucrative routes awarded to weaker carriers. Fares were based on distance in a pattern designed to subsidize short-haul markets by high margins on long-haul routes. Discounts were limited so that competition took the form of service amenities and extra flight scheduling. Such a system had to produce higher prices for consumers, with higher costs and no profits for the carriers. But beginning in the mid-1970s, the CAB carried out a process of piecemeal elimination of all these restrictions. The Airline Deregulation Act of October 1978 phased out CAB authority over routes in December 1981 and over fares in January 1983. In its terminal years, the board allowed even more entry (commencing service within 60 days of application) and exit (90 days' notice on routes with 2 carriers or fewer).

---

[97]Testimony of Chairman John Robson, Hearings on Aviation Regulatory Reform, Subcommittee on Aviation of the House Committee on Public Works, April 18, 1977.

The advent of fully open markets came about just when costs were rising rapidly and the recessions of the early 1980s were taking hold in the economy. High labor costs and the predominance of large, fuel-inefficient aircraft presented the trunk airlines with their worst cash flow prospects since the early 1970s. Their share of domestic traffic dropped from 90 percent in 1978 to less than 75 percent in 1984, while local service carriers offering trunk service grew over the same period to account for the lost percentage points.[98] The trunk and most regional airlines adopted hub-and-spoke route systems that brought passengers from dispersed origin points in smaller aircraft to central locations to be dispersed on dense routes to their final destinations in the largest aircraft. They adopted computer information and pricing systems allowing them to offer many more prices for much more widely varied services.

Both the hub system and computer-based pricing together gave the trunk carriers the strategic means to respond to competitive entry on their established routes. But at the same time, the local carriers and new entrants took advantage of their (nonunion) lower labor costs and of the fuel efficiencies of newer aircraft by targeting more price sensitive markets with lower fares. Consumers responded favorably to these new services and fare variations.

Fare structures in the deregulated industry better reflected the costs of operations. Short-haul fares increased, while long-haul fares declined, as expected from reversing the intentional regulatory underpricing and overpricing of those respective markets. As long-haul fares declined, carriers focussing on tourists and other discretionary services realized higher load factors. While the higher short-haul fares must have reduced passenger demand, there have still been consumer gains from those policy changes. Call and Keeler found a substantial increase in the diversity of prices, with coach fares rising 25 percent (inflation adjusted) between

[98]Kaplan (1986), pp. 40–77.

1977 and 1981, but only 27 percent of passengers traveling at such fares in 1981 as compared to 61.5 percent in 1977. This pricing diversity represented "a movement toward multi-product competition" with the discount fares "reinforce[ing] the market segmentation achieved by new entrants or the lower costs of using wide-bodied jets in denser markets, or the lower prices for one-stop rather than nonstop flights."[99] Consumers also gained through increased availability of discounts, higher frequencies, and better timing of flights. According to Morrison and Winston, improved frequency of flights in short-haul markets resulted in as substantial welfare gains to passengers by 1983 as those from fare reductions in long-haul markets.[100]

The supplanting of regulation by open markets in the airline industry did not cause the industry to conform more quickly with the perfectly competitive model. Bailey, Graham, and Kaplan did find that most prices were within 10 to 20 percent of competitive levels.[101] But there are now advantages for the larger trunk airlines that have hub dominance in gate and landing slots and that have put their computer reservation systems into the most travel agencies at those hubs. Even so, the new diversity in service allows consumers to trade off price and convenience. "All consumers have benefitted as increased operating efficiencies have combined with discount pricing policies."[102]

### Natural-Gas Production

Field gas price regulation had been much more restrictive than airline regulation and, as a consequence, gas markets had a greater distance to go to achieve efficient market per-

[99]Call and Keeler (1985), pp. 241–247.

[100]Morrison and Winston (1985), pp. 57–61.

[101]Bailey, Graham, and Kaplan (1985).

[102]Bailey (1988), pp. 12–46.

formance. Gas shortages in the early 1970s were as large as 20 percent of total demand and were increased by the crude-oil price spirals of the mid-1970s. As demand shifted to gas, unregulated intrastate prices rose and gas supplies were diverted away from price-controlled interstate sales. Volume in the interstate pipelines fell from 14.2 trillion cubic feet in 1972 to 11.9 in 1975 and continued to decline to 10.9 in 1977, at a time when demands were increasing rapidly.[103] Regulation and the resulting secular decline in production were the main features of behavior in field markets for natural gas in that decade.

Deregulation was extremely complicated; the decontrol procedure was set out in legislation that broke down controlled prices into numerous categories and controlled the phasing out of those controls in each category. But with each increase of 50 cents in field prices, costing consumers $0.5 billion in the first year, there was considerable political resistance to decontrol. Congress had to consider not only the great gains from reducing shortages, but also its political losses from substantial price increases levied on existing consumers not experiencing the shortages. The first step was taken by the agency itself in Federal Power Commission Opinion 770 (1976), which allowed increases in new contract field prices of almost one dollar per thousand cubic feet (MCF). Such a price hike, impolitic five years earlier, was justified by estimates of costs for additional supplies that were based on the experience in unregulated intrastate markets.

---

[103]Only part of the demand growth was ever registered on gas markets, however, because regulated curtailments prevented attachment of consumers to delivery systems, and without attachment there could be no indication of willingness to take gas. Even so, if only to maintain existing 1972 demand in later years, those on the pipeline systems should have had three to four trillion cubic feet more than was available over the period 1972–78 (as indicated by total delivery curtailments announced by the Federal Energy Regulatory Commission in the 1977–78 heating year). On various conservative measures, excess demands made up at least one-quarter of total demand in the late 1970s.

Such forward looking estimates were approved by the court in *American Public Gas Company v. Federal Energy Regulatory Commission* (FERC) (555 F2d 852, 1977), which affirmed the authority of the regulatory agency to use the cost estimating procedures of its choice just so long as it provided due process for all parties.

With the price cap lifted by the agency, Congress then passed the Natural Gas Policy Act of 1978 (NPGA). The myriad special provisions in the NGPA protected rights to fixed prices on existing sales, but allowed new contract prices to rise to whatever pipelines would pay. With buyers' competition focused on these new supplies, the new prices had to clear excess demands at higher than long-term equilibrium levels (in fact interstate curtailments were quickly reduced, leaving only very limited shortfalls by 1980 for industrial consumers in certain specific heating markets). Indeed, surpluses developed over the 1980s. Supplies were expanded in response to the deregulated new prices on just new sales, but demands were held back by slow industrial growth and falling oil prices. As availability exceeded the amounts sought by retailers and industrial users, cutbacks in production went into place, particularly in contracts with the highest prices. The control of the deregulation process was so prolonged, as well as so mistaken in its classifications of supply, that it could not succeed.

This process also went too far in allocating sales. The NGPA provided that supplies under existing contracts at the old prices be assigned first to residential customers, with the new prices either rolled in for averaging purposes or paid by commercial and industrial consumers. As a result home-consumer demands were increased beyond levels consistent with a uniform price level in open resale markets, and industrial demands were over prices so as to be shifted to other fuels.[104]

Both airline and natural-gas deregulation showed the im-

[104]Lower demand growth may also have been the result of regulations in the Power Plant and Industrial Fuel Use Act of 1978 and the Energy Supply and Environmental

portant role of commission initiatives. Congress followed the lead of the agencies in deregulating. By selectively decontrolling certain aspects of the process, the agencies and then Congress reduced the sudden impact of the changes brought about by shifting to open markets. But phased deregulation was prolonged and in the case of gas led to even worse results than no deregulation. Congress showed that the decontrol process could make reform indistinguishable from disruption.

## Reform of Health and Safety Regulation

New policies constituting real change have come from three sources—changed procedures, more substantive court reviews, and the adoption of new market mechanisms. They are based on new premises to the effect that regulatory practices have to demonstrate better results than any direct alternative. Three examples indicate that reform has been underway even in the newest agencies.

### Impact Statements

The Ford and Carter administrations both proposed that major agency rule makings be justified on economic efficiency criteria. The Inflation Impact Statement (Ford) and the Economic Impact Statement (Carter)[107] set in place pro-

Coordination Act of 1974. To be sure, the impact of these has been difficult to determine. But the two acts required that electric generating and industrial steam plants not expand operations using natural gas as boiler fuel and that new plants be built with coal boilers. Even so, gas fired plants have not been shifted to coal, nor have gas boilers been moved to standby operations and replaced by new base-load coal plants. New capacity dedicated to coal and nuclear fuel has come on line very slowly because more stringent price regulation has prevented the accumulation necessary for capacity expansion.

[107]Presidential Executive Orders 11821 (expired December 1977) and 12044 (issued March 27, 1978).

cedures whereby agencies had to demonstrate that there
would be reductions in accidents, illnesses, or injuries to compensate for cost increases from new regulations. The agencies, including EPA, OSHA, and NHTSA, have been required
to make such findings in terms of economy-wide impact as
part of their procedures.

In theory, this development of a new process should reduce, perhaps even eliminate, excessive regulation. Any impact statement that found the agency unable to produce positive economy-wide gains would be the basis for denying
implementation of standards. In practice this has been done
only to a limited extent. In the case of OSHA's safety standards for coke ovens in the steel industry, the Council on
Wage and Price Stability (COWPS) completed an Inflation
Impact Statement in the mid-1970s. COWPS differed with
OSHA on the impact of the rules by finding a significant
adverse effect on the economy from the new standards.[108] In
the case of NHTSA regulations requiring air bags in automobiles, the decision process was opened up to allow estimates
of impact on the cost of driving by the automobile manufacturers and the insurance companies. While the impact analyses did not deter NHTSA rule making, they did compel the
agency to take account of the economy-wide effects of rule
makings and to defend this accounting. These and further

[108]On February 27, 1976, OSHA released an inflation impact statement regarding
emissions from coke ovens. The statement estimated that, for final demand, personal
consumption expenditures would rise between .01 and .07 percent because of the
new emissions standards. The study foresaw an increase in federal government
defense spending of between .02 and .11 percent. Federal government spending for
nondefense purposes was projected to rise at least .02 and at most .10 percent as a
result of new standards (*Inflation Impact and Analysis of the Proposed Standard for
Coke-Oven Emissions*, 29 CRS 1910.1029, OSHA, p. 110). "These estimates have been
obtained by calculating Laspeyres price indexes for each of the final demand sectors.
This was done by taking a weighted average of price relations for the individual
industrial sectors producing output for delivery to final demand. The Laspeyres
index for personal consumption expenditures is comparable to the Consumer Price
Index prepared by the U.S. Department of Labor, Bureau of Labor Statistics" (p.
109).

cases indicate that impact statements hinder further development of ineffective and costly equipment standards, even though they have not yet been sufficiently incorporated into decision making to make regulation more effective in general.[107]

### Reform by Court Decree

Federal court decisions evaluating the health and safety control process have been central to the process of reform. Since regulation was established, the courts on appeal of agency rule makings determined the fairness of proceedings and whether there was factual support for agency decisions in the record. This practice encouraged the building of lengthy dockets, but did not much affect the results of the agency process. In four OSHA cases during the 1970s, however, the federal judiciary began to evaluate the results from rule making.

The four court decisions involved OSHA's benzene, coke-oven-emission, vinyl-chloride, and asbestos-dust standards. Each standard specified certain air pollution emissions limits

---

[107]On December 7, 1976, the Council on Wage and Price Stability and Office of Management and Budget issued "An Evaluation of the Inflation Impact Statement Program." The authors pointed out that "those who develop major regulations often pay little attention to economic analysis, at least initially. However, they are aware that at some point in the later development of the proposal economic analysis will be a 'necessary hurdle.' This awareness, which has been sharpened by the IIS (Inflation Impact Statement) program, appears to have some effect on their efforts to identify alternatives and to assess costs" (p. iii). The evaluation, however, found that this effect varied from agency to agency. At the EPA, "the IIS program, coupled with significant internal support, has succeeded in getting decision-makers to be more sensitive to economic analysis" (p. 51). The study found disagreement as to whether or not the IIS program had any measurable impact at OSHA. The authors do note that "the IIS program had resulted in OSHA's paying attention to both the cost and benefit sides as opposed to just considering the costs to firms or adverse effects to employment" (p. 73). Though there were some problems with the IIS program, the evaluation concluded that the program was a success and should be continued: "The IIS program facilitates more rational decisions on proposals whose impact on the economy is substantial. It should be retained and strengthened" (p. 84).

and was part of the set of new rules for health conditions in the workplace. When the asbestos standard went to review, the court upheld consideration of "economic feasibility" as a criterion for the promulgation of the standard.[108] At the same time, however, the court limited its review of the impact of the standard for fear of infringing upon policy making in the agency. The coke-oven and vinyl-chloride standards were reviewed as well, and again the court decisions essentially stopped short of reviewing the economic impact of the standards.[109] In its decision on the benzene standard, however, the court made a significant departure from this position by explicitly using its own cost-benefit criterion to appraise the standard.[110] The court broke through its carefully preserved judicial distance in the previous cases and asserted itself directly in appraising the worth of the standard.

The issues were first raised in May of 1977 when OSHA published a benzene standard that provided for a reduction in the airborne permissible exposure limit from 10 to 1 parts per million (PPM) and established requirements relating to exposure monitoring, medical surveillance, labeling, and record keeping. This proposed standard was based on the determination that employee exposure to benzene presented a leukemia hazard and should be limited to the lowest feasible level. After holding hearings, OSHA promulgated the new benzene standard in February 1978. The American Petroleum Institute filed for review of the standard in the Court of Appeals stating that the evidence did not show that this reduction of the exposure limit was reasonably necessary to provide safe or healthful employment.

In response to the petition, the court held that the reduc-

---

[108] *Industrial Union Department, AFL-CIO v. Hodgson,* 499 F.2d 467 (1974).

[109] *American Iron and Steel Institute v. OSHA,* 577 F.2d 825 (1978), and *Society of Plastics, Inc. v. OSHA,* 509 F.2d 1301 (1975).

[110] *American Petroleum Institute v. OSHA,* nos. 78-1253, 78-1257, 78-1486, 78-1676, 78-1677, 78-1707, 78-1745, slip op. at 80 (Fifth Cir., Oct. 5, 1978).

tion from 10 to 1 PPM was to be set aside, "in the absence of substantial evidence indicating that measurable benefits to be achieved by the reduction of permissible exposure to benzene bore a reasonable relationship to the one-half billion dollar cost of such regulation for the affected industries."[111] It was also decided that the prohibition against human contact should be set aside since the regulation was based on "dated, inconclusive data" and not on the latest scientific information.

The court noted in its decision that, although the statute required health and safety protection for the employee, "it does not give OSHA the unbridled discretion to adopt standards designed to create absolutely risk-free workplaces regardless of cost."[112] In determining whether the benzene standard was reasonably necessary to protect workers from a hazard, the court was guided by the decision in *Aqua Slide 'N' Dive Corporation v. Consumer Product Safety Commission.* The Aqua Slide case, according to the court, "requires the agency to assess the benefits in light of the burdens to be imposed by the standard. Although the agency does not have to conduct an elaborate cost-benefit analysis, it does have to determine whether the benefits expected from the standard bear a reasonable relationship to the costs imposed by the standard."[113]

Noting that OSHA had attempted to measure the expected costs of the standard, the court went on to determine that it had failed to show expected benefits to balance against these costs. Rather, OSHA had assumed that the benefits would be appreciable and achieved at a cost the industry could absorb. OSHA had "based this assumption on a finding that benzene was unsafe at any level and its conclusion that exposures to lower levels of toxic materials would be safer than exposure to higher levels was deficient." Given to failure to estimate

[111]Ibid., p. 80.

[112]Ibid., p. 90.

[113]569 5.2d 831 (Fifth Cir., 1978).

expected benefits, the court argued that "the required support is lacking to show reasonable necessity for the standard promulgated."[114]

This decision could require the agencies to prove that their standards had net benefits to the economy. Another circuit court has made the determination of benefits a direct responsibility of NHTSA as well. The case involved a braking system for trucks and buses established by NHTSA's FMVSS 121, as originally adopted in January of 1973. This ruling established standards for air-brakes in terms of maximum stopping distances for vehicles at different speeds. Although the standard did not specify the technology to be used, it implied that an antilock device was necessary for large trucks in order to meet the requirement that stops be made without lockup of wheels more than momentarily, and the available device consisted of a computer attached to each axle of the tractor-trailer that sensed when a wheel began to lock and temporarily released the brake to regain traction. Serious questions arose as to the reliability and safety of this computer device, because of relay valve failures and false warning signals when used. Radio frequency interference caused the antilock device to malfunction and the brakes to fail without warning. Not infrequently drivers attempted to solve these problems by simply deactivating the device.

In a court test of these standards, Paccar Corporation and the American Trucking Association (ATA) contended that they did not meet statutory requirements of practicability given the high cost of the system and that reliable performance was beyond the reach of current technology. They also argued that the antilock system created a potentially more dangerous situation than faced by vehicles with the old brake systems. The truck brake case was decided in April 1978 in favor of Paccar and the ATA with the court holding that "in view of substantial evidence that performance of vehicles

[114]Ibid.

equipped with a brake anti-lock was not consistent with performance required by the standard and may have been more hazardous in performance than prestandard vehicles, the agency's failure to conduct more intensive testing of vehicles certified under the standard was an illegal abuse of discretion." On appeal, NHTSA argued that the role of court review was more limited than exercised in this opinion and that "the decision in this case amounts to a substitution of judicial for administrative judgment in a manner repeatedly condemned by this court and other courts of appeal." That position was denied by the Court of Appeals. NHTSA subsequently published a notice in the *Federal Register* stating that the no-lock portions of the standard were invalidated insofar as they applied to trucks and trailers.[115]

The OSHA and NHTSA reviews redirected these agencies away from rule making requiring equipment on feasibility grounds to those justified on the grounds of improved results, such as accident reduction, improvement in health, and greater product quality. Whether such measures can be translated into economic benefits is problematic. But having to make estimates of lives saved or products rendered more useful establishes the foundation for a more effective regulatory decision-making process. By adopting the court's line of reasoning, these agencies could reduce the high-cost, low-benefit results from health and safety regulation focused on equipment requirements.

### New Market Mechanisms

By the late 1970s the EPA had demonstrated a remarkable lack of success in implementing the state plans to reduce air pollution. Many states did not have plans, the oldest plants in states with plans did not have control equipment, and there

---

[115]*Paccar Inc. v. National Highway Traffic Safety Administration* (1978); petition for writ of certiorari, U.S. Supreme Court (October term, 1978), p. 14. *Federal Register,* vol. 43, no. 203, pp. 48, 648–49.

were gaps in the supposedly uniform "new" plants standards across the states. By the late 1980s, without going into the question as to whether equipment requirements would eventually reduce pollution, the agency and Congress moved in another direction.

The new argument was that performance should replace equipment requirements on air pollution discharge. The EPA was to allow plants to cap their plant-wide emissions and to seek a future combination of equipment and operating system changes that would achieve an emissions limit at a lower cost. Few plants chose that option in the 1980s—less than 300 registered with EPA according to Hahn and Hester (1989). But many plants chose to offset new emissions associated with increased output by reductions elsewhere in that plant, which is in accord with this first step in regulation of plant performance.

The next step was to put direct controls on specific plant emissions. The Clean Air Act Amendments of 1990 set severe limits by plant on emissions of sulphur oxides for 1995 at the major power plants. These amounts would be licensed and could be traded from plant to plant up to the limit; any overage would be fined as well as taken out of the subsequent year's allotment. The effect of these limits on the industry and economy was not estimated. Indeed, it was no more than the sense of Congress that technology existed to reduce by half the current level of sulphur emissions and that doing so would improve human health. But the changes in regulatory method predictably result in filling the gap in the market system that creates externalities by authorizing purchases and sales of pollution discharge rights.

Markets have not yet developed in offsets and rights because transactions costs are high and property rights are still not sufficiently well established. By putting in place a cumbersome certification process for any transaction of an emissions credit, the EPA has managed to generate costs in excess of prices. Trade under the 1990 amendments would have to take place on the premise that the traded pollution discharge level would not be cancelled by new regulatory standards applied to the seller (taking back the credit) or the buyer (preventing use of the purchased credit). The act states that, while tradeable, pollutant emissions are not property rights of the plant licensee.

### The Sum of the Reform Measures

To count on impact statements or on rights trading to reform the major social regulatory agencies would be unrealistic. The changes made in the agencies to date have had no more than initial, insignificant results. But taking all the radical proposals together would make it likely that there would be substantial reform of the current costly and ineffective process of controlling externalities.

The Clean Air Act would justify performance (emissions) standards on grounds that they result in economic benefits greater than the costs in production of meeting them. Much the same justification would have to underlie the OSHA and NHTSA statutes. The agencies would only set performance standards after generating impact analyses that could meet court evidentiary requirements. They would allow companies to meet such standards by buying performance units from other companies (in part by reducing uncertainty about future rights to tradeable permits). While concrete results cannot be foreseen, the effects will likely lead to a more productive market system.

## More Radical Regulatory Reform

Improving the present condition of the regulated industries could very well require much more than new processes in the agencies.

Because price regulation still uses past-period estimates of costs to establish future revenues, companies inevitably have to price without concern for current costs and demands. Because health and safety regulation centers on uniform equipment standards, regulatory costs have been the same across companies and have been passed on uniformly to the consumer in price increases. But regulation has allowed exceptions across companies in order to protect the least safe and most polluting from closing. As a result, the process necessarily has not had any general impact on ambient and workplace conditions.

Three kinds of radical change would end this condition. The first, in price regulation, would invoke ceilings on price changes based only on current inflation rates and productivity changes at the margin for providing service. The second, also in price regulation, would deregulate industry entirely whenever regulatory practice cannot justify itself against the alternative of an imperfect market. The third, in health and safety regulation, would be to set taxes on externalities, given that the likely economic results could be no worse than the current effects from agency regulation.

The establishment of price caps would eliminate the complex and detailed controls on rates of return (except once a decade, when prices issued have to be brought in line with costs). In the context of regulation as now practiced, the agencies would permit a tariff increase when requested, subject only to the finding that the percent increased did not exceed economy-wide inflation minus that industry's productivity gain rate in excess of the economy-wide average. Reviews of proposals for tariff increases would occur within the year and would use data on actual inflation and productivity. Such a procedure would be, in fact, the same as that used by the FCC to control the price level on interstate long-distance telephone service for AT&T after mid-1990. This method would eliminate the adverse effects of regulatory lag in case reviews, but more importantly, by use of contemporaneous data on costs and demands, would eliminate the process of keeping prices down in periods of high economy-wide inflation.

The second proposal is that the elimination of regulatory controls started in the 1980s should continue in the 1990s. Railroads, airlines, and gas-producing companies are now operating virtually without regulation on services in interstate markets. Deregulation logically should be extended to eliminate substantial parts of state regulatory agency control of the local communications, energy utility, and transportation companies. The legislation to do so should specify a decontrol objective and set general guidelines for the steps to be taken in the decontrol process. The primary objective would be to replicate the results from deregulation achieved at the federal level. Rate controls that have increased costs of service and persisted after new technologies have made competition possible would be abolished.

The further institutionalization of performance standards is the most important step that can be taken in improving health and safety regulation. This not being done would justify a radical turn towards replacing regulation with taxation of externalities. The Clean Air Act Amendments of 1990 imposes such taxes as fines on excess emissions. This process need only be extended to taxing licensed emissions, with the agency making the administrative assessment and the Treasury Department collecting the charge on each unit of discharge. While politically difficult (see Crandall, 1988), this would be the step to take before abandoning this regulation, along with price regulation, and for the same reason.

In recent years, all presidents and most members of Congress have promised to bring an end to excessive regulation. Members of the House and Senate have acted on these commitments by initiating decontrol in particular industries, by calling for termination processes to apply to all regulatory agencies, and by requiring agencies to show that their rules were beneficial to the economy as a whole. But little has come of these proposals, and the question for the 1990s is whether statute reform will be possible.

From all appearances, regardless of the abundance of reform rhetoric, the answer is that such changes are unlikely. The case for reform has been that regulation should be reduced or eliminated to promote efficiency and thereby to add to capacity and output growth. But this requires higher utility prices and lower expenditures on safety or health control equipment in manufacturing. As such, it would be resisted by numerous political interest groups, as a matter of course, even though these changes would benefit consumers (their ultimate constituency) some years hence.

In the 1990s, the American economy will probably continue to be regulated much as it is now. As a result, the economy will not perform well as it realizes continuous reductions in the rates of growth of the quantity and quality of goods throughout the economy. Those goods and services provided by the industries most affected by health, safety, and environmental regulation will be more expensive, less satisfactory in performance, and less likely to improve over time.

The future of the regulated industries does not make the outlook for the rest of the economy promising. Reduced growth in the energy, distribution, and communications industries increases costs of manufacturing and trade, causing their growth rates also to be reduced. Reduced growth in the metals, materials, and automobile industries from health and environmental regulations slows down those sectors of the economy and, since they provide inputs used elsewhere, the rest of the economy as well. Without significant benefits in more safety or better health to compensate for the rising costs of such regulation, regulation will continue to drag the economy down. To continue regulatory practices along the present lines is likely to deprive producers and consumers without much in return beyond legal process.

# Appendix A

Annual Case Decisions of the Federal and
State Regulatory Agencies
(1962 = 1.0)

| Industry | 1969 | 1973 | 1981 | 1988 |
|----------|------|------|------|------|
| Electricity | 1.0 | 3.3 | 6.8 | 1.8 |
| Gas retailing | 0.5 | 4.3 | 5.2 | 1.6 |
| Telephone | 4.0 | 13.8 | 16.5 | 4.2 |
| Airlines | 4.0 | 1.0 | 1.1 | na[a] |

Source: These estimates were compiled from the *Annual Report on Utility and Carrier Regulation* (various years), National Association of Regulatory Utility Commissioners

[a]na = not available

# Appendix B

Rate Structure in the Regulated Industries, 1960–1987

| Industry/Index | 1960 | 1969 | 1973 | 1981 | 1987 |
|---|---|---|---|---|---|
| Electric | | | | | |
|   Industrial/residential | .40 | .44 | .49 | .69 | .62 |
| Natural gas | | | | | |
|   Industrial/residential | na[a] | .30 | .36 | .70 | .54 |
| Railroad | | | | | |
|   (Base = 1970) | na[a] | na[a] | 101 | 271 | 260 |
|   Coal | na[a] | na[a] | 108 | 194 | 133 |
|   Farm products | na[a] | na[a] | 107 | 206 | 185 |
|   Chemicals | na[a] | na[a] | 116 | 259 | 301 |
| Telephone | | | | | |
|   Interstate/intrastate | na[a] | na[a] | 1.00 | .91 | .54 |

Source: Electricity and gas: Energy Information Administration, *Annual Energy Review* and *Natural Gas Annual* (various years); Railroad: Department of Transportation statistical series (various years); Telephone: United States Bureau of Labor Statistics, Producer Price Indices.

[a]na = not available

# Appendix C

## Service Quality in the Regulated Industries, 1960–1987

| Industry/Index[a] | 1960 | 1969 | 1973 | 1981 | 1987 |
|---|---|---|---|---|---|
| **Electric** <br> (Base = 1960) <br> Expected capacity margin | 100 | 77 | 83 | 122 | 111 |
| **Natural gas** <br> (Base = 1958) <br> Reserve capacity | 90[a] | 63 | 54 | 49 | 49 |
| **Railroad** <br> (Base = 1965) <br> Serviceable cars | 100 | 104 | 103 | 101 | 99 |
| Boxcar turnaround time | 95 | 93 | 97 | 70 | 78 |
| **Airline** <br> (Base = 1960) <br> Load Factor | 100 | 85 | 88 | 98 | 105 |
| QSI | na | na | 100 | 108 | 117 |
| **Telephone** <br> (Base = 1958) <br> Dial tone delay | 140 | 84 | 250 | 392 (1977) | na[b] |
| Trouble reports | 96 | 82 | 82 | 94 (1977) | na[b] |

Source: Electricity: Edison Electric Institute, *Electric Power Survey* (various years); capacity margin = $(IC - PL)/IC$. Gas: American Gas Association, *Gas Facts* (various years) and U.S. Department of Energy, Energy Information Administration, *Natural Gas Annual* (various years). Reserve capability equals ratio of natural-gas reserves to annual gross production; deliverability capability equals annual deliverability surplus to annual sales. Railroad: Railroad Association, *Railroad Facts* (various years) and ICC, *Annual Report.* Freight loss and damage index is equal to the freight loss and damage divided by operating revenues; turnaround time is adjusted by average haul per ton divided by train speed. Airline: CAB, *Air Carrier Traffic Statistics and Financial Statistics* (annual). Load factor is the ratio between available seat miles and total revenue passenger miles; quality service index (QSI) methodology (Lottig) is presented in an appendix. Telephone: AT&T internal reports.

[a] in 1961

[b] na = not available

# Bibliography

Aman, Alfred C. and Howard, Glenn S. "Natural Gas and Electric Utility Rate Reform: Taxation through Ratemaking?" *Hastings Law Review* (May 1977): 1085–1157.

*American Iron and Steel Institute v OSHA,* 577 F. 2d 825 (1978).

*American Petroleum Institute v. OSHA,* nos. 78-1253, 78-1257, 78-1486, 78-1676, 78-1677, 78-1707, 78-1745, slip op. at 80 (Fifth Cir., Oct. 5, 1978).

*Aqua Slide 'N' Dive Corporation v. Consumer Product Safety Commission* 569 5.2d 831 (Fifth Cir., 1978).

Bailey, Elizabeth E., Graham, David R., and Kaplan, David P. *Deregulating the Airlines* (Cambridge MA: MIT Press, 1985).

Bailey, Elizabeth E. "Price-Service Quality Diversity in Deregulated Airline Markets," *Advances in the Study of Entrepreneurship, Innovation, and Economic Growth* 2 (1988): 13–44.

Bartel, A. P. and Thomas, L. G. "Direct and Indirect Effects of Regulation: A New Look at OSHA's Impact" *Journal of Law and Economics* 1 (April 1985): 1–25.

*W. Y. Sung v. McGrath, 339 US 33* [*1950*]. "Blackouts on East Coast are called Unavoidable," *Wall Street Journal,* February 28, 1990.

Call, Gregory D. and Keeler, Theodore E. "Airline Fares, Deregulation and Market Behavior" in *Analytical Studies in Transport Economics,* ed. A. F. Daugherty (Cambridge: Cambridge University Press, 1985) pp. 221–47.

Caves, Richard E. *Air Transport and Its Regulators: An Industry Study* (Cambridge, MA: Harvard University Press, 1962).

Caves, Richard E. "Direct Regulation and Market Performance in the American Economy," *American Economic Review* (May 1964): 172–81.

*Commonwealth Edison Company v. ICC,* U.S. Court of Appeals (District of Columbia 76-2070 1989).

Conant, Michael. *Railroad Mergers and Abandonments* (Berkeley: University of California Press, 1965).

Cooke, W. N. and Gartski, F. "OSHA Plant Safety Programs and Injury Reduction," *Industrial Relations Review* 245 (1981).

Cramden, R. C. "The Effectiveness of Economic Regulation: A Legal View," *American Economic Review* (May 1964): 182–91.

Crandall, R. W., Gruenspecht, H. K., Keeler, T. E. and Lave, L. B. *Regulating the Automobile* (Washington, DC: The Brookings Institution, 1986).

Davidson, R. E. *Price Discrimination in Selling Gas and Electricity* (Baltimore: Johns Hopkins University Press, 1955).

DiPietro, Aldona. "An Analysis of the OSHA Inspection Program in Manufacturing Industries, 1972–1973." Draft technical analysis paper, U.S. Department of Labor (August 1976).

Donaldson, Lufkin and Jenrette Securities Corporation. *Domestic Trunk Airlines: A Shortage Industry in the Making* (New York, June 1976).

Douglas, G. W. and Miller, J. C., III. *Economic Regulation of Domestic Air Transport: Theory and Policy* (Washington, DC: The Brookings Institution, 1974).

General Motors Corporation. "Impact of Government Regulations on General Motors." Paper provided through private correspondence (August 1977).

*Industrial Union Department v. AFL-CIO Hodgson*, 499 F.2d 467 (1974).

Jackson, Raymond. "Regulation and Electric Utility Rate Levels," *Land Economics* (August 1969): 372–76.

Jordan, William A. "Producer Protection, Prior Market Structure and the Effects of Government Regulation," *Journal of Law and Economics* (April 1972): 151–76.

Joskow, Paul L. "The Determination of the Allowed Rate of Return in a Formal Regulatory Hearing," *Bell Journal of Economics and Management Science* (Autumn 1972): 118–40.

Joskow, Paul L. "Inflation and Environmental Concern: Structural Changes in the Process of Public Utility Price Regulation," *Journal of Law and Economics* (October 1974): 291–327.

Kaplan, Daniel P. "The Changing Airline Industry" in *Regulatory Reform: What Actually Happened*, ed. Leonard Weiss and Michael Klass (Boston: Little Brown, 1986) pp. 40–75.

Levin, Richard C. "Regulation, Barriers to Exit, and Railroad Investment Behavior." Paper presented at the National Bureau of Economic Research conference on public regulation, Washington, DC, December 15–17, 1977.

Levin, Richard C. "Railroad Rates, Profitability, and Welfare under Deregulation," *Bell Journal of Economics* (Spring 1981): 1–26.

Littlechild, S. C. and Rousseau, J. J. "Pricing Policy of a U.S. Telephone Company," *Journal of Public Economics* (February 1975): 35–56.

MacAvoy, Paul W. *The Economic Effects of Regulation: The Trunkline Railroad Cartels and the Interstate Commerce Commission 1870–1900* (Cambridge, MA: MIT Press, 1965).

MacAvoy, Paul W. *Explaining Metals Prices* (Norwell, MA: Kluwer Academic Publishers, 1990).

MacAvoy, Paul W. "The Record of the Environmental Protection Agency in Controlling Industrial Air Pollution," in *Energy, Markets and Regulation,* ed. R. L. Gordon, H. D. Jacoby, and M. B. Zimmerman (Cambridge, MA: MIT Press, 1986). pp. 107–36.

MacAvoy, Paul W., ed. *OSHA Safety Regulation: Report of the Presidential Task Force* (Washington, DC: American Enterprise Institute for Public Policy Research, 1977).

MacAvoy, Paul W. and Joskow, Paul L. "Regulation and the Financial Condition of the Electric Power Companies in the 1970s," *American Economic Review* (May 1975): 295–301.

MacAvoy, Paul W. And Noll, Roger. "Relative Prices on Regulated Transactions of the Natural Gas Pipelines," *Bell Journal of Economics and Management Science* (Spring 1973): 212–34.

MacAvoy, Paul W. and Robinson, Kenneth R. "Losing by Judicial Policymaking: The First Year of the AT&T Divestiture" *Yale Journal of Regulation* 2 (1985): 225–62.

Manne, H. G. and Miller, R. L. eds., *Auto Safety Regulation: The Cure or the Problem?* (Glenridge, NJ: Thomas Horton, 1976).

Mendeloff, John. "An Evaluation of the OSHA Program's Effect on Work-place Injury Rates: Evidence from California through 1974." Report prepared for the United States Department of Labor (July 1976).

Moore, Thomas G. "The Effectiveness of Regulation of Electric Utility Prices," *Southern Economic Journal* (April 1970): 365–75.

Morrison, Steven A. and Winston, Clifford. *The Economic Effects of Airline Deregulation* (Washington, DC: The Brookings Institution, 1986).

Myers, Stuart C. "The Application of Finance Theory to Public Utility Rate Cases," *Bell Journal of Economics and Management Science* (Spring 1972): 58–97.

National Association of Regulatory Utility Commissioners. *Annual Report on Utility and Carrier Regulation* (Washington, DC, 1988).

Nelson, James C. "The Effects of Entry Control in Surface Transport" in *Transportation Economics* (New York: The National Bureau of Economic Research, 1965) pp. 381–422.

Nichols, A. L. and Zeckhauser, Richard. "Government Comes to the Workplace: An Assessment of OSHA," *The Public Interest* (Fall 1977): 39–69.

Noll, Roger. "The Economics and Politics of Regulation," *Virginia Law Review* 57 (September 1971): 1016–32.

*Paccar, Inc. v. National Highway Traffic Safety Administration,* 573 F.2d 632 (1978).

Peltzman, Sam. *Regulation and Automobile Safety* (Washington, DC: American Enterprise Institute for Public Policy Research, 1975).

Peltzman, Sam. "The Effect of Safety Regulation," *Journal of Political Economy* (July–August, 1975): 677–725.

Peltzman, Sam. "Toward a More General Theory of Regulation" *Journal of Law and Economics* 19 (1976): 211–40.

*Phillips Petroleum Company v. Wisconsin,* 225 US 625 (1954).

Pierce, R. W. "Using the Gas Industry as a Guide to Reconstituting the Electricity Industry" *Columbia Law and Economic Studies* Working Paper 35 (1989).

Robertson, Leon S. "A Critical Analysis of Peltzman's 'The Effects of Automobile Safety Regulation,'" *Journal of Economic Issues* (September 1977).

Rohlfs, Jeffrey. *Economically Efficient Bell System Pricing,* Attachment H. AT&T's submission to Congressman T. Van Deerlin, October 31, 1978.

Salomon Brothers. "Electric Utility Regulation Semi-Annual Review," (New York, August 1, 1990).

Sands, Paul E. "How Effective is Safety Legislation?" *Journal of Law and Economics* (April 1968).

*Society of Plastics, Inc. v. OSHA,* 509 F.2d 1301 (1975).

Smith, Robert S., *The Occupational Safety and Health Act* (Washington, DC: American Enterprise Institute for Public Policy Research, 1976).

Smith, Robert S., "The Impact of OSHA Inspection on Manufacturing Injury Rates," *Journal of Human Resources* 145 (1979).

*St. Joseph Stockyards Company v. United States,* 298 US 38 at 49–50.

Stigler, George J. and Friedland, Clarice. "What Can Regulators Regulate?" *Journal of Law and Economics* (October 1962): 1–16.

Staff paper, "An Economic Evaluation of the OMB Paper on the Costs of Regulation." Proposed for the Subcommittee on Oversight of the Commerce Committee, September 1975 (Washington, DC: U.S. Government Printing Office).

Twentieth-Century Fund, *Electric Policy and Government Policy* (New York: Twentieth-Century Fund, 1978).

*Universal Camera Corporation v. NLRB,* 340 US 474 (1951).

U.S. Comptroller General, *Effectiveness, Benefits and Cost of Federal Safety Standards for Protection of Passenger Car Occupants* (Report to the Committee on Commerce of United States Senate, CED-76-121, July 7, 1976).

U.S. Council of Economic Advisers, *Economic Reports of the President* (1976).

U.S. Council of Economic Advisers, Economic Reports of the President (1978).

U.S. Council on Environmental Quality, *Annual Report* (Washington, DC: U.S. Government Printing Office, 1976).

U.S. Department of Commerce. National Highway Safety Agency. *Annual Report of the National Highway Safety Agency* (1967).

U.S. Environmental Protection Agency, Office of Air, Noise, and Radiation, Office of Air Quality Planning and Standards, *Air Quality Data—1972 Annual Statistics*, EPA 450-2-74-001 (March 1974).

U.S. Environmental Protection Agency, *National Air Quality and Emissions Trend Report, 1976* (Research Triangle Park, North Carolina, 1976).

U.S. Environmental Protection Agency, Office of Air Quality Planning and Standards, *Air Quality Data—1979 Annual Statistics*, EPA 450-4-80-014 (September 1980).

U.S. Environmental Protection Agency, Office of Air Quality Planning and Standards, *Annual Assessment of Air Pollution*, EPA-45014-81-014. (February 1981): Appendix A.

U.S. Geographic Survey Circular 715, *Water Quality Assessment with Application to the Willamette River Basin, Oregon* (1977).

*W. Y. Sung v. McGrath*, 339 US 33 (1950).

White, Lawrence A. *The Regulation of Air Pollutant Emissions from Motor Vehicles* (Washington, DC: American Enterprise Institute for Public Policy Research, 1982).

U.S. National Highway Traffic and Safety Administration. *Motor Vehicle Safety, A Report on Activities Under the National Traffic and Motor Vehicle Safety Act of 1966 and the Motor Vehicle Information and Cost Savings Act of 1972*, January 1, 1975–December 31, 1975, Order No. DOT-HS 801 910 (Washington, DC: U.S. Government Printing Office, 1976).

U.S. Occupational Safety and Health Administration. *Inflation Impact and Analysis of the Proposed Standard for Coke-Oven Emissions* 29 CRS 1910.1029.

Weiss, L. W. "State Regulation of Public Utilities and Marginal Cost Pricing" in *Case Studies in Regulation: Revolution and Reform*, ed. L. W. Weiss and M. W. Klass (Boston: Little, Brown, 1981).

Wellisz, Stanislaw. "Regulation of Natural Gas Pipelines: An Economic Analysis," *Journal of Political Economy* (February 1963): 30–41.

Lawrence J. White. *The Regulation of Air Pollutant Emissions from Motor Vehicles* (Washington, DC: American Enterprise Institute for Public Policy Research, 1985).

Winston, Clifford, et al. *The Economic Effects of Surface Freight Deregulation* (Washington, DC: The Brookings Institution, 1990)

# Index